PSALMS OF LOVE

(A Book of Verses)

The One Truth of Bible, Quran & Vedas

ANTONY THEODORE
&
TAPAN KUMAR PRADHAN

Edited by

Dr Tapan Kumar Pradhan

Copyright© 2021 Kohinoor Books
All rights reserved.

ISBN : 978 – 81 – 952546 – 1 – 3

First Edition 2021

Printed and published by

KOHINOOR BOOKS
www.kohinoorbooks.com

Kohinoor Star Publications Private Limited
MI-622, Pocket-6, Sector-A10, Narela, New Delhi – 110 040

CONTENT

PART-II : Songs of the Mystic

PART-III : Lament of Heart

PART-IV : Paeans of Love

PART-V : Soul's Songs

PART-VI : Prayer Talks

PART-VII : Songs of Silence

PART VIII – Hymns of God

EPILOGUE

ACKNOWLEDGEMENT

I owe a debt of gratitude to my fellow poet friends on Poemhunter website. Most of these poems were first posted on the poemhunter platform where they got enriched by the comments and criticism of countless poetry lovers. My poetic craft has been shaped by the honest feedback received from thousands of readers on such online platforms. Although I have published my poems on several websites, it is on poemhunter.com that I received wholehearted support from many kindred souls.

Dr Tapan Kumar Pradhan offered to present my poems in a book form. Many years ago I had requested Dr Tapan to write a few poems for me. I had also once requested him to gift a book of his choice to me. He had promised to me both. I think he has far exceeded my expectations. I have discussed with him several of my poems at length. I have also discussed with him the underlying unity among all major world religions including Christianity, Hinduism and Islam. I believe that he shares my thoughts on the relevance of Christ's teachings for the modern world. I have full faith in his capacity to honestly interpret my poems.

"ANTONY THEODORE"

FOREWORD

This book contains 197 poems spread across eight interwoven parts. All the poems are themed on Jesus Christ and his 'timeless teachings. But the book is not limited to Christianity as a religion. Rather these poems explore universal truths in Christ's sermons which are the same as the truths contained in other ancient scriptures like the Quran and Vedas. These truths are applicable to every human civilization in all ages.

The poems draw inspiration from the Psalms, which are an integral part of the Christian Bible. Psalms are nothing but musical rendering of the musings on God by ancient mystics like Solomon and David. The truths of Psalms also find echo in the Veda, Upanishads and Quran. 'Therefore each poem included in this volume can be interpreted from the perspectives of Hindu, Christian, Islamic and other religious philosophies. By reading and comparing the footnotes given below each of the poems, the reader can appreciate the inner spiritual messages contained therein. All these poems are highly symbolic, just like the ancient scriptures were. The cat, dog, bird, beast, flower and tree mentioned in the poems do not refer to physical plants or animals, but rather to aspects of cosmic realities. In this way, these poems contain the essence of all world scriptures.

Antony Theodore is a spiritual poet. Although he has written extensively on the scriptures of all major world religions, his meditations on Christ have been most revealing and uplifting. Many of Antony's poems are already scattered over the internet in various forms. This book is a humble attempt to bring some of the best amongst Antony's spiritual poems under a single comprehensive framework. I have selected these poems on the basis of their immediate relevance to the broad theme and structure of this book. These need not be the most representative of Antony's immense poetic oeuvre. Some of the better known poems by Antony have already been published under two other edited titles by me, viz. "Jesus Christ In Love" and "I Am Your Baby, Mother". The increasing popularity of these poems is testament to the enduring relevance of Antony's poetry in contemporary world literature.

In many of the poems included in this book, the poet has provided footnotes to throw light on the original inspiration behind their composition, as well as the scriptural and historical background of the theme. I have added in the footnotes a few relevant verses from the Vedas, Upanishads, Qur'an and Bible to illustrate the inner spiritual messages. Occasionally I have also provided additional footnotes to drive home the spiritual ramifications of a particular poem. My notes essentially contain my personal views from my scholastic vantage point, and need not reflect the poet's original view on the matter.

Almost all the poems have been edited by me to conform to the overall design of the book. Some poems were originally in free flowing passage form. These have been modified and tweaked slightly so as to have a more presentable verse form. Some abbreviations have been expanded and some unclear words have been removed. However the original essence behind the works has not been compromised with. I have been in close correspondence with the poet for almost a decade. I have discussed both poetic techniques as well as scriptural interpretation with the poet over hundreds of fruitful hours. So I have reason to believe that I intuitively understand the poet's point of view behind these timeless creations. I am thankful to the poet for allowing me the liberty to freely explore and interpret these spiritual gems.

Some of the poems contained in this book have appeared in slightly different versions on various websites and online platforms. Antony has also been editing and tweaking the poems online from time to time. However, I am presenting the poems as received by me from the poet during my extensive correspondence. The original psalms in the Book of Psalm had detailed superscriptions providing comments and musical directions. But in this book the poems have footnotes describing the spiritual undercurrents and thematic context of the text.

Tapan Kumar Pradhan, EDITOR

ANTONY THEODORE
Life and Works

Readers worldwide have been intrigued by Dr Antony Theodore's inspiring poems on humanity, religion and spirituality. Antony's poems offer amazing clarity and insight into many cryptic messages contained in ancient world scriptures such as Bible, Gita, Veda and Qur'an. The poems are rather simple but original, and they contain the underlying essence of all world religions. Without preaching any particular doctrine, the poems contain universal messages of brotherhood and love.

Who is Antony Theodore?

Dr Antony Theodore has legions of followers on various online poetry platforms. On Poemhunter website Antony is one of the topmost popular poets in the English speaking world, consistently appearing among Top 500 world poets. Thousands of fans worldwide have read and commented on the unique and insightful spiritual gems penned by "Antony Theodore".

According to legends and hearsay Dr Antony was born as John Antony Theodore Vazhakoottathil in Alleppey district of Kerala, India. After he was orphaned in early childhood, he was nursed by his devout Catholic godmother Genova Ma. After Genova's untimely demise Antony migrated to Germany. He studied at Ludwig Maximilian University in Munich and Fordham University in New York. He reportedly obtained two bachelor's degrees in science and business administration, and later on obtained two doctoral degrees in English literature and Philosophy of World Religions.

In 1986 when he was travelling from India to Germany, Antony's flight carrying 400 passengers got hijacked at Karachi airport in Pakistan. He survived with four gunshot wounds, while 22 of his fellow passengers were killed in the 17 hour long siege. This traumatic experience turned his mind to poetry and social activism. He was ordained as a pastor and served as a chaplain in St Martin, Munich. Antony remained unmarried and spent a large part of his life in Dortmund, Germany.

However, the diligent and inquisitive readers might have already guessed that actually there is no such poet as the Christian Poet Dr Antony Theodore in the physical world in the 21st century. There is no such poet in Germany as claimed in many websites. One Fr Antony Theodore is listed in the Diocese of Alleppey, and one Pastor Antony Theodore Vazhakoothathil in listed in the pastoral team of Dortmund. The list of persons injured in the 1986 Pan Am flight hijack at Karachi (en route to Frankfurt from Mumbai) also contains a person named Father Anthony Theodore. However none of these persons correspond to the poet writing under the pseudonym of Dr Antony Theodore aka Tony Brahmin on Poem Hunter and myriad other poetry websites. When I first came across Antony's poems on internet, I did extensive search online to identify the person. A careful scrutiny of the poems clearly points to the poet's Indian roots and family connections with the Kashmir province of India.

Hemangi Sharma as Tony Brahmin

Dr Antony Theodore is none other than the Indian mystic poet Hemangi Sharma from Kashmir. This is a truth which was known only to me till date. This is because Hemangi Sharma never liked to publish poems under her own name. She has various reasons for doing so. Hemangi has written thousands of poems under hundreds of different pseudonyms such as Lalitha Iyer and Poet Poet etc. Antony Theodore is her pseudonym or fake ID under which she has published her interpretation of Jesus Christ's universal teachings on Poemhunter and other digital platform. In routine online correspondence with fellow poets, Antony Theodore invariably uses the nickname Tony Brahmin, which reflects Hemangi Sharma's Indian origin as someone born in a traditional Kashmir Brahmin family.

In the Appendix to this book I have provided details of Hemangi Sharma's poetic works under various pseudonyms on poemhunter and other websites. Further details on Hemangi Sharma's extraordinary relationship with me can be found in my book *I, She and the Sea*.

What is Antony's Religion?

Antony Theodore primary writes on Christian values. In her poems the birth, wanderings, teaching, suffering, crucifixion and resurrection of Jesus Christ have been tellingly re-enlivened. However "Antony" does not profess any particular religion. Her poems bring forth the universal truths common to all world religions. Therefore Antony is as much a Hindu and Muslim as she is a Christian, Buddhist and Confucian. Although the poems contained in this book are inspired by Book of Psalms of Christian Bible, they will readily find echo with the mantras of Vedas, Upanishads and verses of Qur'an also.

INTRODUCTION

The Book of Psalms has been an integral part of the Christian Bible since ancient Jewish tradition of worshipping God. Original psalms were hymns to God in musical form. The New Testament has references to psalms as prayers recitations in praise of God. However many psalms contain general moral instructions. Meditation on the psalms is regarded as one of the highest form of devotion invoking divine presence into human life.

Most of the psalms have been attributed to King Solomon and David, although there is no clear historical evidence that they were the real authors. But the fact that psalms have been included in both the Old and New Testament indicates that they have been inspired by Jesus Christ's teachings. Even if psalms existed before the birth of Jesus the Messiah, the message contained in them align with the sermons of Christ.

Jesus in his physical human form graced this earth for a brief period of thirty three years at the beginning of the modern Christian era. The four books of the New Testament of Holy Bible throw light on only the birth, infancy and the last few years of his ministry. The Gospel is silent on the intervening years of Jesus's extraordinary life. However the record of his teachings as gleaned from those few years of his life have had a profound impact on the shaping of world history. The momentous impact of that one human life is still being felt in the unfolding of human civilisation. That extraordinary impact emanates from the purity, truth and love manifested in the unblemished life of Christ.

Jesus used to speak to his disciples in the ancient Aramaic language, while the original psalms were in Hebrew language. The teachings have been carried forth by apostles and missionaries to the furthest corners of the world through hundreds of translations and re-translations in several different languages. However, much of the original teachings have been distorted and lost through the translations.

For instance, we may take the expression "Word of God" in Bible. Its exact equivalent in Vedic Sanskrit is "Shabda Brahman" – i.e. Word-God. It may be noted that Shabda in Sankrit has two meanings – Word as well as Sound. In the original Aramaic version, Word of God would have symbolised the primordial sound of creation (Aum-Amen-Amin) which permeates the entire universe. However, translated into modern English, Word merely connotes the written word as a combination of letters of the alphabet. Similar is the case with other Biblical expressions like Bread, Wine, Fish, Star, Flesh etc. In the original Aramaic/Hebrew the meanings would have been quite different from what they ordinarily connote today. If we take the original meanings, we shall find that all the scriptures of world religions essentially speak the same One Truth.

There are many pointers in ancient scriptures to indicate the essential unity of all world religions. For instance the Psalm verses of Bible and Sama mantras of Veda have in-built instructions for their correct incantation. Both are meant for devotional outpouring rather than knowledge dissemination. Just like the Psalms are to be sung with music, the mantras of Sama Veda (साम वेद) are to be melodiously intoned. Even the similarity between the words Psalm and Sama is too obvious. Similarly, for Hindus Brahma is the primordial primogenitor of all human beings, while all Abrahamic religions (e.g. Judaism, Christianity, Islam) trace their origin to a common patriarch named Abraham. The words Abraham and Brahma have almost the same sound, and hence the same hoary origin (the ancient Sanskrit root "BRI" / वृ means "to expand" or to become many out of one). Abraham's wife was named Sarah, who was also known as his sister. They had their first offspring Isaac when they were aged 100 and 90 respectively. Similar is the case with Brahma, whose wife Saraswati was created out of his body splitting into two. Hence Saraswati can be conceived of as Brahma's daughter, sister as well as wife all rolled into one! All the ancient rishis of Hindu faith were "mind born" offspring of Brahma-Saraswati. Just like Abraham was 100 years old when he became a father, Hindu iconography also shows Brahma as a very old man with white beard and his consort Saraswati as always adorned in whites. The names Sarah and Saraswati are quite similar. From this it is evident that Brahma and Abraham symbolically represent the differentiation of one universal spirit into several branches of knowledge, science, arts and several species of animals and plants.

However the present book does not attempt to dig out the original meanings of scriptures through phonetic or lexical re-interpretation of currently available texts. It merely acknowledges that inner meanings of scriptures can be quite different from the surface meaning of written text. Poems contained in this volume are expressions of the original truth of all religions as perceived by the poet. Words like bird, cat, dog, wings etc mentioned in these poems are therefore highly symbolic and do not pertain to mere physical beings. Rather they correspond to various aspects of eternal cosmic reality. A bird flying across the dawn sky towards the golden horizon is symbolic of the human soul's striving for God realization. Antony Theodore's poems delve much deeper than the surface meaning of Biblical teachings. They dwell on the universal message of love and brotherhood contained in the Gospel, which is the same as that expressed through the Vedas, Gita, Quran and other world scriptures.

The poems in this volume have been arranged under eight parts. They start with physical creation of plants, birds and animals, and gradually progresses through finer evolution of human consciousness until it reaches the stage of silent prayer and inner communion with God.

The first part titled "Songs of the Wild" contains poems based on analogies and themes taken from the animal kingdom. On a metaphysical level this symbolises the descent of universal spirit to earth in the form of countless individual souls. The birds, beasts, plants and flowers mentioned in the poems are all symbolic. For instance, the poem "God, Give Me My Wings" describes different body organs of the bird as representing different aspects of the cosmic being "Viraat Purusha" ((विराट पुरुष) as extolled in the Upanishads.

The second part dwells on Songs of the Mystic. King Solomon and David, to whom most of the Psalms have been attributed, were mystics of the highest order. But similar mystical experiences have been reported by saints and sages of all religions as can be seen in the poem "Poet Mystic".

The third part titled "Laments of Heart" deals with the pangs of separation that a human soul feels for its missing other half. "Two Hearts" and "I Wish I Could Enter Your Heart" depict the yearning for divine re-union.

The fourth part is titled "Paeans of Love". By loving another human being one expresses love for the Supreme Lover present in all hearts. Marriage of a man and woman is a mundane expression of that divine love. "Lust Trap" and "One Flesh Love" glorify the covenant of devoted union.

The fifth part titled "Soul's Songs" deals with soul to soul communication on supra-physical plane. The poems "Soul Marriage" and "My Soul Mate" express divine longings and spiritual aspirations.

The sixth part is titled "Prayer Talks". Poems in this part are more in the form of instructions on meditation rather than songs for chanting. Poems like "Advaita Mukti", "Vedarita", "Buddha Mudra" and "East and West" show the inner unity of eastern and western religious traditions.

The penultimate part titled "Songs of Silence" describes the nature of inner communion in silence. "The Silent Desert" and "Whisper Last Night" show the possibility of highest realisation through silencing of the human mind.

The last part "Hymns of God" signals complete surrender of the fruits of one's action to the Almighty Creator. This is the highest level of human consciousness as depicted in "Hand of God" and "God Alone".

PART – I

SONGS OF THE WILD

BIRDS AND ANIMALS IN LOVE

AND A BABY IS BORN

Truth is naked. Truth was, is and will ever be. But we humans like to wear masks.

To perceive pure love that is God, you have to unmask your heart, unmask your soul, unmask the purity of your being.

Mind, reasoning and all sensory knowledge are only stumbling blocks in realising the pure purity of being. When you realise this simple truth, you give up all thinking. And when you give up thinking the ugly clothing will fall down. The naked cabaret dancer will start dancing. Beauty will flow, hearts will smile, penetrating your being with knives and organs made of pure energy. Then a little baby you will become. Like amoeba, you are the mother, you are the kid.

For when God's light opens my heart, I hear the laughter of innocence in my being.

ROSE IN LOVE

The rose once grew
and fell in love
with morning rays
of the glorious sun

Waiting through whole night
she danced in rapturous joy
when morning's first light
gave birth to dawn

Mildest and sweetest were the first rays

Rose kissed the honey rays
and wished to plunge deep
into the mild light
of the rays she loved

When evening came
sun burst into riotous colors
on the crimson horizon
and then vanished in the sea
dropping like a dead stone
and then the rose cried
falling into depressive sadness

Ah new dawn will come
Live in hope, and wait
for the birth of new dawn
with its wondrous rays of light
Wait my child, do not weep
Wait for the coming Dawn.

LIFE ON A PALM LEAF

Big leaf
small leaf
budding leaf
ripe old leaf
brown and red
yellow and green
soft and tender
subtly lined
stern and brittle
veined sharp with riddles
palms of nature lie on dust
trample them not
they are hidden story chests

what beauty, what modesty
unlike a flower they don't show off fragrantly
neither do they bed with golden honeybees
silent messengers, they are discreet maps
to nature's origins and ways
every leaf with enigmas profound
sleeps silently under the heaped garbage
the grandpa leaf, mama leaf with world of nature
engraved in their palms - legendary historians
they have the bond of life still vibrant within
harping in their hearts are a tree's legend
big leaf, small leaf, tiny leaf, broad leaf
red and green and yellow and brown
they are nature's love in modesty's gown.

"The righteous man will flourish like the palm tree. He will grow like a cedar in Lebanon."
(Psalm 92.12)

ROSE, MANGO, BREADFRUIT TREE

There are in the world
three types of men:
those resembling the rose,
the mango and the breadfruit tree

The one bears only blossoms,
the second both flowers and fruits
and the third only fruit

The one talks,
the second talks and acts,
and the third only acts,
but says no word.

Do not ruin your fame
by unnecessary bragging.

Poet's Note :- Wisdom received from reading Lanka Kanda of Ramayana epic.

"He will be like a tree firmly planted by streams of water. Which yields its fruit in its season. And its leaf does not wither. And in whatever he does, he prospers." (Psalm 1.3)

"He who made for you from the green tree, fire, and then from it you ignite." (Surat Yasin 36.80)

PRETTY ROSE

Pretty rose tree, pretty rose tree
Why don't you give me a rose today?

Rose showed me only her thorns

Are you jealous, Rose
that I have another rose
fixed on my coat button?

Pretty rose tree kept silent,
showed me only her thorns,
and looked at the chattering sparrows
not caring for my presence

Pretty rose, pretty rose
are you jealous, jealous
that I have another rose
fixed on my coat button?

"I am the **rose** of Sharon, a **rose** of the valley" (Song of Solomon 2.1)

"When the sky was torn apart, it was like a red **rose**, like ointment." (Surah ar-Rahman 55.37)

FOREST JASMINE

I smelled the forest jasmine,
wild but profound in its perfume
my bones filled with the perfume
spread on my being
to wake me from my dreams

I heard the silent music of night
and felt it kissing my lips softly
In my heart there were rhythms
unheard of before

My limbs moved
to a song and its rhythms
and I felt the softness of petals
of the sweet smelling jasmine.

FLOWER IN ME

The flower in me
looks for light

Me the flower,
wants to bathe
in God's light

It is in God's
mysterious silence
I like to live

I find all my answers
in this silence with Him.

"He who understands the flowers of water, becomes the possessor of flowers, children and cattle. Moon is the flower of the water. He who understands this fact, becomes the possessor of flowers, children and cattle. (Taittiriya Arayanaka 1.22)

SUNFLOWER LOVED A GLOWWORM

Once,
Sun flower fell in love
with a glowworm

The tiny fly flew slowly
spreading tiny light
in the darkness

The sunflower, even when
it adored the sun
kept in her heart
a love that is pure
for the glowworm of night.

In the darkness
when sun went beyond horizon,
she remained dreaming
of the glow worm
and hoped the tiny little firefly
will come and land
on the soft petals
of the sunflower one day

She chanted a noble song
The fire of the heart
of the sunflower
burned in the silence of night.

The sunflower in the night
lay in repose
imagining the beauty

of the glowworm.

One night
as sunflower slept
indeed came the glowworm,
landed on the soft petals
of the sleeping sunflower
emitting radiant light.

The tiny glow worm slept
on the soft petals
of the sunflower
that night.

Even in sleep
the glow worm gave
the sun flower its light
free of cost, out of sheer joy.

God above saw it and smiled
and the angels sang
and the saints played
on their golden harps.

"But I am a worm and not a man - a reproach of men and despised by the people." (Psalm
22.6)

FLOWER AND BUTTERFLY

Can a butterfly ever forget
the scent of the flower
and sweetness of the nectar
which it sucked in intimacy?

I saw a little butterfly
playing on the flowers
in my terrace garden

It was so lovely
I looked at it
and I watched
how playful it was

the butterfly forgot itself

Butterflies are like poets
They forget themselves
very very often

Do you hear O poetess and poet
the butterfly and the flower
it kissed and sucked,
singing together
an addictive lullaby every night?

"For he knows how we are formed, he remembers that we are dust. The life of mortals is like grass, they flourish like a flower of the field; the wind blows over it and it is gone, and its place remembers it no more." (Psalm 103.15)

BUTTERFLY, FLOWER AND SNAIL

Once a butterfly, a flower
and a snail met together

Butterfly said :
I am colorful and I can fly
Flower said :
I bloom and I have fragrance

Snail told simply
and in a satisfying tone :
I am satisfied with myself as I am.
The thought that God loves me
as I am
is enough for me.

I am very happy.

"But the rich should take pride in their humiliation – since they will pass away like a wild flower." (James 1.10)

"God loves those who are steadfast" – Qur'an (3:146)

BE LIKE THE ANT

Wise men are always at work
Do not waste your time
on Netflix, playing video games

If you don't want poverty
you must develop a strong work ethic

Be like the ant

"Go to the ant, O sluggard;
consider her ways, and be wise

Without having any chief,
officer, or ruler,
she prepares her bread
in summer and gathers
her food in harvest

When will you arise
from your sleep?

A little sleep,
a little slumber,
a little folding
of the hands to rest,
and poverty will come
upon you like a robber,
and want like
an armed man.

"Go to the ant, thou sluggard; consider her ways, be wise." (Proverb 6.6)

ANT AND THE BEE

An ant I saw
searching for food
a grain I dropped
it took it in mouth
and happily went.

I saw the bee
buzzing around flowers
soon its hive was filled
with the gardens looted
and nectars potted
bees have finished
their life's missions

I saw the waves
lustfully lashing
the rocky terrains
greedily washing
the golden sands
again and again they came
to plunder the shore
and pirate its wealth.

Every being has a mission
what is mine I wonder
just forget and concentrate
not on awareness of Knowledge
but Awareness of Being.

"The ants are a people not so strong, yet they prepare their meat in the summer." (Proverb
30.25)

SAILOR'S PARROT

A mariner had a sweet parrot
He used to smoke cigars
and loved to pump out white puffs
like smoke from tall chimneys
He enjoyed smoking.

One fine morning
the parrot began to cough
and coughing became severe

So the captain took it
to the Veterinary doctor

Doctor tested it thoroughly
"Your parrot does not suffer
from psittacosis, sir
or pulmonary inflammation

It is only imitating your cough".

Self-discovery.

Editor's Note :- Almost all human afflictions are self-inflicted. This is not only a scientific discovery, but also a truth contained in all scriptures.

"Like a bird that strays from its nest is a man who strays from his home." (Proverb 27.)

LOVE BIRDS

Lovebirds, O hold hands
till the warmth spreads all over
Rub your little beaks
till you feel the silence of love
Hug now and hug again
till the soft little feathers fall
Cling together and dream a sweet dream
till the shy smile conquers the dream.

Editor's Note :- Real love is experienced in complete silence and not through talking minds.

"I know all the birds of the hills, and all that moves in the field is mine." (Psalm 50.11)

WOUNDED LITTLE BIRD

I saw on the pathway
a wounded little bird

I took it carefully
kept it warm
inside my palms,
came home
fed it with milk

It was lovely to see it
drinking slowly
the milk of love i gave.

Then kept it safely
in a small box
in the wool bed
and we both slept

The next day
i repeated into its ears:
fly, fly, fly, learn to fly again.

Weeks passed by.
Every day we both sang
the same song
fly, fly, fly, learn to fly again.

Today i saw it flying
from my room
to the wide world
of butterflies and birds.

OH NIGHTINGALE

Oh Nightingale, Nightingale
Would you sing me a song
full of melody?
The poet asked.

'Mellifluous' do you mean?
The Nightingale asked
"Yes" said the poet with a smile.

"I have forgotten all my songs"
The Nightingale answered

Why? The poet asked.

"My heart is full of sorrow
I cannot sing now
I have forgotten my songs
Would you forgive me dear Poet? "
said the nightingale
in a voice full of sadness.

Poet was so sad
he began to write songs
to bring the nightingale
to sing in joy.

"Beside them the birds of the heavens dwell; they sing among the branches." (Psalm 104.12)

LITTLE ROBIN SANG

Little robin sang :
Give me the crumbs
you let fall under the table.

Pick it up
and save it for me
when I fly to you
fluttering my little wings,
give me those crumbs
for my little beaks.

In return I shall sing a song for you
and flutter with my wings in love
when I see you sitting alone
on your silent rock.

"For in vain is a net spread in the sight of any bird." (Proverb 1.17)

BIRDS OF LOVE

From the horizon
they flew down,
the birds of love.

They flew to my heart,
in the garden of my heart
to settle there to teach me
how to love in this mad world.

Their beauty attracted me
So I listened to their chattering
these lovebirds who were keen
to teach me the joys of love.

They told me about beauty of God,
about God's angels and saints
in the world of eternal sunshine.

Birds from that world of love
told me: Love and love alone
can bring you to world of beauty
from which we flew down to your heart.

I simply believed it
and still I remain
in meditation, drinking
of the beauty of the world of love.

"That path no bird of prey knows, and the falcon's eye has not seen it." (Job 28.7)

TAKE ME UNDER YOUR WINGS

You are like a bird with large wingspan
You conceal me under your wings.
I shall find my refuge there.

Do not allow my heart to be proud
Make my eyes not haughty
Reveal your mysteries in secret
When I come to you in prayer
Pleading with a lowly heart.

I humbly implore your majesty
Let me find favour in your sight
I set my soul in silence and peace
Enlighten the eyes of my heart
I bow before you O Lord of Universe.

"The wings of the ostrich wave proudly, but are they the pinions and plumage of love?" (Job 39.13)

MIGRATING BIRD

Like the migrating birds,
man has a homecoming instinct

Fly in, fly in
Zeroing in

In the heart of hearts he knows
that this world is unreal
His unrest deep down in himself
makes him look for the Otherworldly

So the pilgrim seeks
the City Unseen

The Mystics are
path-finders of the Spirit
blessed with spiritual intuition

They tell us about absolute beauty
that lives in the City Unseen.

Editor's Note :- Homecoming instinct refers to longing to return to one's true eternal abode in God - "The Unseen City"

"Look at the birds of the air: they neither sow nor reap nor gather into barns, and yet your heavenly Father feeds them. Are you not of more value than they?" (Mathew 6.26)

SONG BIRD

The song bird sings
Harken !!

The invisible songbird sings
Do you hear it?

Harken ! Harken !

Where is your home my song bird?
The song bird did not answer.

It went on singing and singing
until i heard it
deep down
in my soul.

"The flowers appear on the earth, the time of singing has come, and the voice of the turtledove is heard in our land." (Song of Solomon 2.12)

I ASKED THE BIRD

I asked the little bird on the tree
would you sing a song for me?

sing a song
sing a song

The little bird answered :
If you make me smile
and laugh now merrily
I shall sing a lovely song for you
for i am very sad now.

I need a bit of love
I need a smile
Song will come

For making others happy
is our divine call.

"If you come across a bird's nest in any tree or on the ground, with young ones or eggs and the mother sitting on the young or on the eggs, you shall not take the mother with the young."
(Deuteronomy 22.6)

CORMORANT AND THE BLACK

Who is fair
let us have a test
call the judge
let us play the best
Cormorant plunged into water
and washed and washed and washed
and dived and clapped its wings
and breasts apart hands laid to rest

Man poor trusted his friend
he little did know he is cheated behind
he too fell into water and filled up to his lungs
and swam and swam and swam and emerged a junk
his body glazing with elite whiteness
all black washed away by cleansing water body
and so he lost in the game with Cormorant, fair young buddy.

Do not imitate the bird he said
birds are tricky and funny, he said
man's rules apply to man alone
poor bird was sad that man
lost his weight and colour.

"The little owl, the cormorant, the short-eared owl…" (Leviticus 11.17)

Editor's Note :- This poem was written and posted by Hemangi Sharma on March 10, 2016

WINGED BIRDS ASK COLOUR OF LOVE

Silver is the sky
Green are the leaves
Shining are the waves
Tiny wings of morning bird
Fluttering in the mild wind
Ask me
What is the colour of love in your soul?

Grey are the clouds
Brown is the earth
Blue are distant hills
Winged birds of coloured feathers
Dancing on the merry breeze
Ask me
What is the colour of love in your soul?

Editor's Note :- Bird depicts the undulating human mind attracted to external appearances of transient things possessing many hues and qualities. Soul is attracted only to the eternal imperishable.

BIG BIRD SEEKS INNOCENT JOYS

I wished a kiss from you
I have thirst for forbidden tastes

Shall we hold hands and sit
on the shore of this rivulet
to dream of castles and fairies?

You are a scented flower
Oh, how I love to kiss your petals

I am a big bird
and I carry you on my wings
to the land of spring blossoms

Shall I pour honey on your tongue
and may I lick it from you?

When you giggle
I shall laugh.
When you smile
shall I pinch your nose?

Come let us run on bare feet
on the green grass
racing each other.
I shall then allow you to win the race.

That will be my joy when I go to sleep;
You and me and You win always.

IN SILENCE BIRDS FLEW TO ME

I remained on the island of mercy
all alone in silence.

Birds of joyful love
flew to me
around me
In little circles
to feel my benevolent presence

I saw my shadow
cast like a log
on the lowly water
the water was still,
so was my heart
bereft of will

In the mystic atmosphere
I felt His presence
He told me :
Alone in silence
Can you feel me.

"I looked, and behold, there was no man, and all the birds of the air had fled." (Jeremiah 4.25)

LET MIND BIRDS SING AND FLY

Birds fly
from mind to mind
he reads my mind
definitely with a find

Is it a laser beam
that invisibly shuttle
like the frog's tongue
reaching out others' morgues

If I could read your heart
why should I talk to you,
If I could study your mind
why should I ask you

When mind to mind thing happens
then control will you, control will I
then confusions will fuse
actions profuse

are you then hypnotised
or are you mesmerised
how shall you then travel
in this intangible flight

when minds speak
and matters tweak
oh stop the butcher
let the birds sweet sing.

"For in vain is a net spread in the sight of any bird." (Ezekiel 1.17)

BIRDS OF SUNSET AND SUNRISE

Setting beauty is amazing
sounds of birds warning
and rustle of leaves tired
glow of golden clouds delicate
sun like a dying heroine
soft and delicate shines

Rising Sun has dawn at command
he dictates every dew to dissolve
every bud to bloom readily
reversing their fatigue into singing
birds now greet with sweet melodies
as life beats and the city throbs
sunrise boosts up sleepy knobs.

Sunset sinks into the night:
it has its sweetest moments
nameless love shrouds the sky
silent hearts companies seek
every house cheers up with life
as darkness speaks of silent souls
hugging warm beneath the rugs

Sunrise opens up every privacy
peeps into door, egging on to tour
it fruitifies the nights harvest
into a mini marathon
halted by nights oblivions.

"Truly, I tell you, this very night, before the rooster crows, you will deny me three times."
(Mathew 26. 34)

ARE YOU ALONE MY BIRD

Are you alone my little bird
alone in the vast expanse
of the sky and the sea's shore?

May i come to you to hold your hand
and lead you through the peaceful shore
full of mild light leading you to the cave
of your solaceful praying heart?

There we shall sleep together in love
and in peace, in hugs and in joy

Beauty shall cover us both
to protect us when we hug in silence
in sincere deep love of tenderness
that angels alone possess.

"Even the sparrow finds a home, and the swallow a nest for herself, where she may lay her young, at your altars, O LORD of hosts, my King and my God." (Psalm 84.3)

A FEATHER FLEW TO MY FEET

I prayed to God.

God, i need comfort today
I need to be comforted now

God sent me a feather

Feather flew down to my naked feet

It began to touch my feet
in soft, feathery ways
that only a feather can do

I simply looked at the feather
and my feet, reveling in joy

I smiled

And I was silent.
Feather was silent.

"Look at the birds of the air: they neither sow nor reap nor gather into barns, and yet your heavenly Father feeds them. Are you not of more value than they?" (Mathew 6.26)

NIGHTINGALE FEATHER

I got one day a nightingale feather
I took it to my bed
It was a great treasure
I kept it on my breast
I slept in harmony

In the depth of the night
the feather began to sing
the loveliest of songs
and then my heart sang
With the feather's song
and i slept in peace
It was my eternal sleep.

"He will cover you with his pinions. And under his wings you may seek refuge. For his faithfulness is a shield and bulwark." (Psalm 91.4)

"The left wing of a bird is verily by one feather better. Therefore the left wing is larger by one verse." (Aitareya Upanishad 4.2.5)

GIVE ME MY WINGS

God, give my wings might
Give me the aroma of cheer
Help me to hear the whispers
of my prayerful silent heart
Let the touch of your beauty
make the strings of my soul vibrant.

God, give me a ladder
and send me an angel
to help me to climb up to you,
to your holiest shrine
in the heavens above.

"Vairaja Pranava is the king of birds. Its right wing is the letter A. Left wing is letter U. Its tail is letter M. Its head is the half-sound. Its two legs and tail's tip are the three qualities of man. Its body is Truth, right eye right conduct, left eye wrong conduct. The feet, knees, hip, navel, heart, throat and point between eyebrows are the seven planes of human existence." (Nadabindu Upanishad)

Editor's Note :- Pranava is the primordial sound of creation – Aum/Amen/Ameen. Vairaja refers to Viraat Purusha or the personification of entire created universe.

BEAUTY AND THE BEAST

the mate of beauty
searched for a partner
and found a beast
howling in the forest
she was beautiful
so beauty has no life in her
she wondered if the beast
so powerful yet could be
hers at least.

she mirrored her face
and puzzled went on
what my beauty is to me
if I can't fetch someone strong to fend
The beast was surprised
to win the love of beauty
ugly as its own face was
wild as its passions were
beauty was soft and tender
her feelings very delicate and modest
beast was beastly to say the least
all its emotions battled with zest

how could a beauty beast be
or beastly beauty together could be
ridiculed by the irony of the moment
nature prolonged destiny's consent
and so beauty was enthralled
the fountaining strength of beast she recalled
amazing vitality and courage she breathed
for her the beast was a boosting privilege

beast was honoured
beauty he indulged with decent corners
though he acted for beauty's innocence
still it made no sense for his essence
what drived the maid to crave his presence...

in life too young worlds
are crazy and contrary
they search for things
they do not have
passionate about foreign fashions
and imported sperms
or European Wombs
all that is One's own
one fails to rejoice on own...

"And to every beast of the earth and to every bird of the heavens and to everything that creeps on the earth, everything that has the breath of life, I have given every green plant for food." (Genesis 1.30)

SQUIRREL'S HOME

One day it didst rain
wetting every dust and grain
I lost my dreams
as the cell screamed
halting my trips to lands strange
alerting me to wake up range

I saw a Squirrel
a funny Squirrel
running from nest to chests
chest to nests
of building mounts
to fill up the home
under the roof of sky
with plenty of warmth
to room its booms.

O Squirrel Squirrel
how I long to be
home with thee
a little squirrel

"If the earthen tent we live in is destroyed, we have a building from God, an eternal house in heaven, not built by human hands." (Corinthians 5.1)

"Put your outdoor work in order and get your fields ready; after that build your house." (Proverbs 27)

THE SQUIRREL'S TAIL

How sweet sweet
the little squirrel is
sounding tweet tweet
as it jumps up and down
upon the wires and cords
from roof to roof
as it jumps to seek
some new nuts quick
or some new creek

the way it lashes
its bushy tail
up and down
left and right
beckoning the world
signaling something wild
circussing across the lanes
managing nuts and guts
building its little home
upon the untouchable domes

Today, as I watched
and watched amazed
the lovely little being
with its little teeth
and knify claws
pulled out bundles of cotton yarn
from inside the box of an a.c. torn
wrapping material it seems
the happy kid it was
for it rained harder and harder

poor thing now loved the new wonder
as I viewed it stuffed and stuffed
into its tiny paws
as much cotton as it could
with the balancing legs
and jutting mouth
balling a whole bunch
into something smaller to sponge
what a clever act of life
the whole world of rags
reduced to a global bag
for a sweeter heaven
so nimble, so brainy,
the world of homes
built by cute little forms....

"The Lord will make you the head and not the tail. You shall be above, and not underneath,
if you listen to the command of God and observe them carefully." (Deuteronomy 28.13)

CAT OF MY BEING

I saw the cat
in my inner mind
fondling sweetly
the softest fur coat
I knew she was within me
ages past, when I was born on earth.

I saw the seed
of life sprouting
in the rain wet earth
I could feel the growth
every morning my eyes explored
she has begun the journey to plant
I could feel the tree in a seed
and the seed was lying deep within.

I could feel the globe
the things of beauty
of love and loveliness
all encased within my heart
the flowering gardens
the silky grass
the snowcapped peaks
the supple curves
the saintly caves
the silent innate contains
what the vibrant outside exhibits

All the noisy flamboyant curses
reside in soft silent muses
the statue is contained in the stone

magic is only in your majestic hone
the pen was before,
the paper too
and sky and ocean
birds and the rains
yet, the poem is born
only from the microscopic within
when unseen angels ring the bell
to wake up the cat of my being.

"They wear pride like a jeweled necklace and clothe themselves with cruelty. These fat cats
have everything their hearts could ever wish for." Psalm 73.6-7)

"One day while playing with a cat, Ganesha beat it up in anger. Later when he went to his
mother Parvati, he saw wounds all over her body. 'Who has beaten you, mother', Ganesha
asked. 'My son, you have done this. You beat up the cat. But I am also inside the cat. If you
hurt the cat, you hurt me too."

THE PRAYING DOG

O my friend,
You kneel on the way side
Your dog kneels also
in devout prayer

Does the dog know what is prayer?
He kneels because he knows
his master is in union with God
(I almost cried when i saw his picture)
Are there holy rays of prayer
going out of your bowed head
which your dog understands?

Love, devotion, prayer
faithfulness go together
Your deepest longing
is love and prayer

Affection for all humans
and all that is in nature
and the love of God
go together.

Is it not a wonder
how prayer works?

"The woman said, "Lord, even dogs eat the crumbs that fall from their masters' table." Jesus
answered, "Woman, you have great faith! I will do what you asked." And at that moment the
woman's daughter was healed. (Mathew 15.28)

SONGS OF THE MYSTIC

VOICES FROM WILDERNESS

THREE CRAVINGS

Man has three deep cravings of the self.
These are the three expressions of his restlessness.

Man has the craving in him
to be a pilgrim and a wanderer
It is the longing to go out
from his normal world
in search of a lost home.

The next is that craving of heart to heart
It is the longing of the soul for its perfect mate
which makes him a lover.

The third is the craving for inward purity
and perfection, which makes him an ascetic
and in the last resort a saint.

LIGHT

Under the blue sea
deep down
i sat in a cave.

Cried the whole night
till a beam of light
to wipe my tears

came.

("i" is purposely written in small letters)

Poet's Note :- This was published in Poet Freak under the name of Genovamaaa.
Genova was my beloved mother. She died at the young age of 38. I want to keep
her name alive as long as I am alive.

Editor's Note :- The poet never had a physical mother named Genova. Both her
parents were alive at the time of publication of this book. Hemangi Sharma wrote
and posted this poem on Poemhunter website on July 2, 2016 – the day she lodged
a false complaint against me with the police. The poem clearly appears to be
autobiographical elements.

POET MYSTIC

A true poet is a mystic
And the mystic is on his journey

Allow the mystic to live and look,
then he will speak the language
of immediate union

It may not have clarity of philosophers
for mystics leave mere intellectual sphere
to enter an intimate personal sphere

Absolute of the mystic
is not dry, but alive
attainable and lovable

Mystic's quest is expressed
in symbol of a pilgrimage
under two different aspects

One is a search for hidden treasures
the other is a long hard journey
towards a known and definite goal

O Poets! Come!
Shall we journey together
and accept this mystical way
to attain the goal of our lives?

Poet's Note :- Dante's Divine Comedy is considered as a faithful
and detailed description of the Mystic Way.

INNER SUN

There is an inner sun in me
radiating in and through

It depicts my inner harmony
and it manifests love
spreading rays of light
all around me

It gives me light in my eyes
and a smile on my lips
and joy in my heart

The harmony makes my prayer sublime
to reach the heart of the Highest
The eternal, never ending Unseen One

He conquered me with his love
and he smiled at me
and mystified my soul
with his affection and love

Now I live only for Him
the Lover of my soul
and Lord of Universe
chanting all along
His praises on my lips.

"The sun shall not strike you by day, Nor the moon by night" (Psalm 121.6)
"He is the One Who created day and night, the sun and the moon - each travelling in an orbit." (Quran 39.5)

MOONLIGHT ORCHESTRA

sound of wild brooks
spit by mountain rocks
spelling the silent lives
with syllables of rhythmic beats

drops of rain aching to beat
upon the breast of leaflet wet
audible to only insect sets
incredible to the world
of buzzing electronic sets

at the mid of night
when world is buried asleep
an orchestra of moonlit waves
rocks the seashore paves
beating the bare chest
of unyielding sands
the crazy water bands
spell the dark hours
with mysterious stands.

"Blow the trumpet at the new moon, at the full moon, on our feast day." (Psalm 81.3)

"Blessed is He who has placed in the sky great stars and placed therein a lamp and luminous
moon." (Quran 25.61 - (وَجَعَلَ فِيهَا سِرَاجًا وَقَمَرًا مُنِيرًا)

IN SEARCH OF SUN AND RAIN

In search of sun rays
I went high up the air
all melted I returned
with no trace of mine
but only a clean washed swine.

In search of seas
I went for diving
only water and water
drowned my senses hotter
no truth I could divine.

In search of smell
of earth's treasures
I dug up and up
till my knees plunged
into the heaps of mud
and then the earth worms
spoke of languages new

I wanted to know
how the buds all opened
so I waited all night
and wandered round the garden
to examine every plant
the way it bloomed
past midnight when the breeze blows
pressing eyebrows to sleep, to sleep
i fell asleep without sensing my creep
till breath of dawn woke up me to leap.

MOON COME EMBRACE ME

Love flows with perfect grace
like the dove that wants to fly

I remember her embrace
soft like a whisper

Hold me my desire
oh my heart!

Moon, come bathe me,
caress me.

As feathers of a wing
cuddle together,
I want to cuddle with you
and gaze at your face
with golden light
shining in my eyes.

"And a great sign appeared in heaven: a woman clothed with the sun, with the moon under her feet, and on her head a crown of twelve stars." (Revelations 12.1)

"It is not allowable for the sun to reach the moon, nor does the night overtake the day, but each, in an orbit, is swimming." (Quran 36.40 - لَا الشَّمْسُ يَنْبَغِي لَهَا أَنْ تُدْركَ الْقَمَرَ
وَلَا اللَّيْلُ سَابِقُ النَّهَار)

AND THE MOON SMILED

In tiptoeing tiny steps
I came to you
to pluck your soul

You found me, hugged me
kissed, and squeezed my lips

Then…
you plucked your soul
to give to me
and the moon smiled.

"The moon and stars to rule over the night, for his steadfast love endures forever."
(Psalm 136.9)

"And the moon – We have determined for it phases, until it returns like the old date stalk." (Qur'an 36.39 - وَالْقَمَرَ قَدَّرْنَاهُ مَنَازِلَ حَتَّىٰ عَادَ كَالْعُرْجُونِ الْقَدِيمِ)

BLISSFUL RAIN

Delicate and blissful rain
may fall on you
as blessings of heavens

The gentle rain may stream
down on you to purify you

The little flowers may bloom in you
spreading their lovely fragrance
wherever your feet may lead you

The great rain may refresh your mind
that you become pure like a pristine lake
in which the blue of the sky is reflected
and sometimes millions of stars shine.

These blessings I send to you today
Smile, O lovely one of my heart.

"Breaking open the clouds You create channels for rain! You strike fast the mammoth cloud! Oh Indra! You cast open the mountain of cloud making the showers, destroying the darkness!" (Rig Veda 5.32.1)

"As the rain and the snow come down from heaven, and do not return to it without watering the earth and making it bud and flourish, so that it yields seed for the sower and bread for the eater." (Isaiah 55.10)

"And He sent down, from the rain clouds, pouring water" (Qur'an 78.14 - وَأَنْزَلْنَا مِنَ الْمُعْصِرَاتِ مَاءً ثَجَّاجًا)

STARS OF HEAVEN

Last night
in deep silence
immersed in silence
I stood on top of the hill
and cried loud
"I love you stars
My love is real.
I do love you.
My love is sincere".

Then i saw with my own eyes,
the stars came inside my open palms
My palms were full of light
I remained in peace
Slowly the stars entered
into my body through my hands,
entered into my eyes,
entered into my heart,
entered into my being.

In a moment
I was full of light.

"In the day of the Lord, the stars of heaven shall not give their light and the sun shall be darkened in his going forth." (Isaiah 13:10)

"O my father, indeed I have seen [in a dream] eleven stars and the sun and the moon; I saw them prostrating to me." (Qur'an 12.4)

Editor's Note :- The eleven stars and Sun/Moon represent the twelve spiritual centres in the human spine.

IN THE WILDERNESS

In the wilderness I sit
all alone, all alone
meditating on your wonders

There is only the sky above
Angels watch me when I pray

All else is stone
dead stone
where I sit
motionless

Only in aloneness
can I lift up my heart
and my starved brain
to Lord Almighty

This aloneness
gives me strength
It unites me with the Almighty
Let his Holy Name be praised.

"Immediately the Spirit impelled Him to go out into the wilderness. And He was in the wilderness forty days being tempted by Satan; and He was with the wild beasts, and the angels were ministering to Him." (Mark 1.12)

"Jesus, full of the Holy Spirit, returned from the Jordan and was led around by the Spirit in the wilderness." (Luke 4.1)

I WISH MY NIGHTS WERE LONG

I wish my nights are too long,
when you are gone, as I alone
could dream of you and dance
through in your absence.

I wish my nights are too long,
when you are with me all life,
for then too we could sing the songs
of innocence and love's essence.

I wish you to be a poem
in the stones of my life's path
for then every traveler could marvel
at your beauty and intrinsic charm

I wish you to be my Creator God
for you are my love and eternal cord
I fear not for you shall be within me
till the sun to stars shrink and wink.

I wish, I wish, all the love be for all
like rain, sunshine and maiden breeze
all perfumed and scented with blooms
be pure and soft like the nascent kid.

"That which is night for the worldly people is the hour of awakening for the yogi."
(Gita 2.69)

"The night is far gone; the day is at hand. So then let us cast off the works of
darkness and put on the armor of light." (Romans 13.12)

SPRING SOLILOQUY

To the Spring
I asked :

Wherefrom,
Whereto

You come and go?

She was just silent.

***** ***** *****

His eyes speak to me
I do not hear anything

But my eyes understand

My heart understands
this mysterious language.

***** ***** ******

Lofty in the white
shining dome of skies
I sat inside
my moving palace
and was lost
in soliloquies.

THE MODEST SEED

The seed is shy
so modest it is
it does not show
it is the giant tree
that touches the sky
it spreads branches
shading a battalion
nesting a million
with leaves countless
and fruits immense
loaded with urchins
at topmost branches
swinging and dancing
a house of greens
with mounds of mud
heaped in between
her coiled hairs
rooted deep down with lust
for water and wealth of crust
all fullness endowed
the seed is silent
it never speaks of
its greatness or pride
yet, how cheap we are
we little humans
with little knowledge
verse about secrets of creation
when god in his infinite grace
draws these very lines
upon the electronic face
just to make us happy
and soothen our childish cries.

the sperm little did it know
that egg is going to steam it
and stimulate it to symphony
of the survival of the fittest
just to kindle its urge to reach
and outwit the competing millions
neither the ovum could comprehend
that the silly tailed little being
is such a creative monster
that in one blast it will pursue
and break open its virgin breasts
and the world of wombs
will become a truth of life
that a being of beauty it will confine
in its eternally unfound bounds
going down, oh, going down
reducing self to spermovum mix
some worm wriggles down my spine
and then, and then, ah then
before that, before that, all that
will you share that before I end.

"For truly, I say to you, if you have faith like a grain of mustard seed, you will say to this mountain, 'Move from here to there,' and it will move, and nothing will be impossible for you." (Mathew 17.20)

"Indeed, Allah is the cleaver of grain and seeds. He brings the living out of the dead and brings the dead out of the living. That is Allah; so how are you deluded?" (Qur'an 6.95 Surah Anam - إِنَّ اللَّهَ فَالِقُ الْحَبِّ وَالنَّوَىٰ يُخْرِجُ الْحَيَّ مِنَ الْمَيِّتِ وَمُخْرِجُ الْمَيِّتِ مِنَ الْحَيِّ ذَٰلِكُمُ اللَّهُ فَأَنَّىٰ تُؤْفَكُونَ)

UMBILICAL CORD OF GRACE

We are born with a centre
free in every sense
free of expectations
ambitions and embarrassments
free of fear and worry
It is an umbilical spot of grace
that engulfs us in peace.

Psychologists call it psyche
Theologians call it Soul
Jung calls it seat of unconscious
Hindu Gurus call it Atman
Buddhists call it Dharma
Sufis call it Qalb
Jesus calls it Centre of Love
and dwelling of the Holy Spirit.

Be conscious
of this inwardness
and know what we are

This coming to consciousness
is not discovery of something new
it is a long and painful return
to that which has always been.

"On the day you were born your cord was not cut, nor were you washed with water
to make you clean, nor were you rubbed with salt or wrapped in cloths." (Ezekiel
16.4)

WORLD OF A BABY

Days pass
desires dwindle
rays of light cease
eyes seek glasses

when the lovely little babe
opens into the tiny world
with his black brown looks
when he first sees the twists
and colours of life
little does he know
the day of delight will pass
as ageing sight diminishes
vanishing sights of past

when we see the green plants
and azure sky of lovely pants
little if at all we realise ever
that all the lights at twilight
end up into nothing to sight...

"Behold, children are a heritage from the Lord, the fruit of the womb a reward. Like arrows in the hand of a warrior are the children of one's youth. Blessed is the man who fills his quiver with them!" (Psalm 127:3)

THE MAN WITHIN

there is nothing
in the space between
hormones and habits
reproduces and cohabits

body is flimsy
man inside is the dagger
cloak is powerless
oak within is the manager

I see this body
fenced by fancy looks
my baby embodied
the Newtonic buddy

I see the brain
spark and the light
alert and sound
creativity abound

you are the scientist
you are the sculptor
you are the writer
you are the director

yet, I could only marvel
at the dead body
man who stole the scientist
topped the list
man who stole the sculptor
was ranked first

man who wrote the fate
of the poor writer
he is the perfect mate
man who filmed the drama
he packed up the director

what a marvel!
the dead and the living speak
the coins in your purse
your talents and tons of money
Boss where are you?
who sucked your life
dead one I love you
YOU are the Wisdom
YOU are the Temple
of learning and reality !!!

the mystic man is yet to come out

"Therefore we do not lose heart, but though our outer man is decaying, yet our inner man is being renewed day by day." (Corinthians 4.16)

"Behold, You desire truth in the innermost being, And in the hidden part You will make me know wisdom." (Psalm 51.6)

WOMAN BE THE CROWN

The Bible says :
Man is the head
of God's creation!
If man is the head,
woman must be crown.

When God made woman,
He was finished with His creation.
Woman was the last creative act of God
(You can make of that what you will!)

When Adam went to sleep,
angels made a surgery on his side
and woke up without a real rib
making woman "the backbone".

In all sincerity, a godly woman
is the backbone of the home

Without godly women,
their work, their influence
and their serene abilities,
we would have to shut
the doors of our homes
and declare the home
an unfit place to live.

"It is not good for the man to be alone. I will make the woman to be an authority
corresponding to him." (Genesis 2.18)

GIVE ME A HAND

Give me a hand
give me a blow
give me some sand
let me simply lie low

Give me a heart
give me painful darts
give me some truths
let me writhe in naked woes

Give me an eye
lasering through misty skies
give me a hand
to trace through deserted lands

let me be wise
to see beyond the face
let me be wise
to spell before my life dices.

"If thou wilt take the left hand, then I will go to the right; or if thou depart to the right hand, then I will go to the left." (Genesis 13.9)

CAN YOU HEAL?

Can You heal my wounds?
My heart bleeds incessantly
Would you touch my wounds?

I long for your healing touch

My pride melts into humility
I look at you with pleading eyes

Please touch me and heal me
I need your healing touch.

CAN THE I KNOW ITSELF

Is it possible for a human to know what 'I' is?
We use it almost always

Can the knife cut itself?
Can the tooth bite itself?
Can the eye see itself?
Can the "I" know itself?

WILL YOU COME?

Will you come?

I wait for you in the darkness
sensing the glowing lamp in me

Will you come ???
My heart sighs.

LAST WALLET

The last wallet
we will ever need
is our good works
of love and service

My ability to forget
myself in serving the poor
is the wallet that i need
for my journey to infinity

That alone will count at the end.

LIKE WATER

I wish to be like the water
that moves in the river

I want to be like the water
that meanders through forests

I wish to be like the water
that make the fields fruitful
bringing everywhere life in full.

"And he charged them that they should take nothing for their journey, save a staff only; no bread, no wallet, now money in their purse." (Mark 6.8)

"When I sent you out without a wallet, traveling bag, or sandals, you didn't lack anything, did you?" They replied, "Nothing at all." (Luke 22.25)

RICKSHAW PULLER

I sleep on the roadside
All the shops are closed

No people on streets
I am a rickshaw puller

How shall I earn money?
No one comes to me
to travel with my rickshaw
I cannot buy any food

Here I sleep on the roadside
while the rich sleep in palaces

My plate is a piece of paper
Who will give me food now?

I am hungry and thirsty
in this long lockout
because of corona

Before corona eats me up
hunger will kill me

Will you bury me then?
Where? And how?

"Will the wild donkey bray from hunger if fresh grass is beside him? Will the ox low from distress if it is near its feed?" (Job 6.5)

FEEDING THE DEAD

Why do you offer
food for the dead
feeding the ones
who have no intestine
no stomach to hunger

who asks you
to feed the mouthless ones?
they who know not
the difference between
consumables and non?

who could give any answer clear
to this feeding habit of dead ones dear
if only they could speak
wont they ask things they would take
rather than what we could make

when dead bodies burn
or cremated meet the worm
they transcend to a world
where food and water trouble no more

the dead ones rise
to forms high
as they die
in the spheres of spirits
they become energy rings
that rotate the earth
and revolves the planets

when a grass
you like straw
when a fruit
you go for juice
when a tree
you are free
and when a bird
you are high
up in the sky

tied up you are
when you are a human
as an eating being
upon the earth of living
the higher you transform
your senses evolve
to consume energies
that vibrate in plasmic auras

why feed the spirits
with solid matter?
why feed yourself
with foolish contentment?
love the living, love the beings
with naked heart full of prayers
invoke them to allay your fears.

"The dead will live. Their dead bodies will rise. You who lie in the dust, awake and
shout for joy! For your dew is a dew of light. The earth will give birth to the spirits
of the dead." (Isaiah 26.19)

THE LITTLE HAND

Little hand once said to the big hand :
You, big hand, I need you
because I feel safe with you

I feel your hand when I wake up
and you are always with me
for when I am hungry
it is you who feed me

when you help me to grab
something and build it up
when I try my first steps with you
and if I err I keep looking up

I can come to you 'cause I'm scared

I ask you
stay close to me
and hold me!

Thank God
that you exist for me.

"I am sending an angel before you, to keep you on your way and to be your guide
into the place which I have made ready for you." (Exodus 23.20)

"And he had in his hand a little book open: and he set his right foot upon the sea,
and his left foot on the earth," (Revelations 10.2)

THE CLOSED DOOR

There will be doors
that close before you

When a door closes
preserve hope and faith

Do not worry
Sooner or later
a greater opportunity
will come your way

If the closed door had opened
It would have blocked this new life

This new opportunity presents itself
While the old door closed before you

....

I now understand the mystery
of closed doors and life's path

I await the new opening
with a heart full of hope.

Editor's Note :- I had frequently used the metaphor of closed door while discussing with Hemangi Sharma about her turbulent past life.

"Jesus came, though the doors had been barred, and stood among them and said – 'Peace to you'." (John 20.26)

TRUTH IS NAKED

Truth is naked
Moon is naked
Elephant is naked
and so is the ant
the tiger
the butterfly
the monkey.

Adam and Eve were naked
and all angels in paradise
and so was the creation
only because
truth was always naked
It is and it will always be.

As years went by
Humans invented dress,
learned thus to hide the truth.

Capitalists made industries
calculated all the profits
advertised how good it was
to cover the naked truth.

And they created slaves
made use of poor workers
of third world countries
to create dresses of all fashions.

They saved money in the banks
all over the world.

Alas! One day the capitalist
suffered heart attack and fell
banks profited from his money

The miserable dress makers
in the factories remained poor
and died cold in their misery

Truth is naked
Truth was naked
Truth will always be naked.

"And he said, I heard thy voice in the garden, and I was afraid, because I was
naked; and I hid myself." (Genesis 3.10)

NAKED BEAUTIES

When thoughts are naked
Truths are born
When words are naked
Silence is born

When objects are naked
Light passes on
When sky is naked
Spring is born

When earth is naked
Deserts are born
When hearth is naked
Hunger is born

When clouds are naked
Droughts are born
When shrouds are naked
Corpse are strawn

When words become naked
Meanings dance upon
When world becomes naked
Creator descends again

Naked beauty is very strong
Untouched it penetrates
and upon touch
Life's mystery awakens...

"And they were both naked, man and his wife, and were not ashamed." (Gen 2.25)

MASKS

Tear away
all your masks

Cast away
all falsities

Be clear
like a crystal

Be a mirror
unto the world.

"The face of truth is covered behind a mask of gold. That thou remove, so that truth eternal I may perceive." (Isopanishad 15)

"And the eye of the adulterer watches for the twilight, thinking, 'No eye can see me,' and covers his face with a mask." (Job 24.15)

WHO WILL QUENCH MY THIRST

Morning brings a new song
from beyond the world of skies
where the angels and saints live

this new song reminds me to pray
and praying white swans I see
chattering prayers of sparrows I hear

With gentle care I kneel
and thank with folded hands
drubbing all the dogmas
lost in my own cogitations
about God and the world beyond

I walk through the mystery path of flowers
and chuckle quietly in stealth
while angels count my footprints

Who can build a bridge
from earth to heaven?

Deep in my innermost recess
I know my soul is thirsty
to attain the divine

Who will quench my thirst?
Who will build my bridge?

"Standing in the water I am thirsty. Quench my thirst, Lord." (Rig Veda 7.89.4)

"Whosoever drinketh of this water shall thirst again." (John 4.13)

ONLY YOU, MY BELOVED

In the presence of my beloved
there is no sin nor virtue
no darkness no light
no philosophy no theology

There are only flowers
and fruits without trees
only a radiant shine
but no austere life
there is no knowledge
no place, no space
there is nothing but you
only you are present
my beloved

Only You.

"Leave all other paths and take surrender in me alone." (Gita 18.66)

Poet's Note :- i knelt down in prayer. i had a deep sense in me that my heart loves God. But it is a God who is beyond all religions and religious concepts. i do not know how to express it in words. Here i am with my poem. Hope the reader understands my struggle to put into words my mystical sense.

LOVE YOUR DREAMS

Love your dreams
Love to dream

Dance in the moonshine
Sing on the seashores

Fly with the wings of eagle
Soar high in the skies

Talk with the moon
Talk with the skies
in their slow flight

Sit on the rainbow

Smile like a peacock's heart
when it dances unawares

See the humble heart
of the beggar on the street
imitate his humility

Feel with the poor
let your eyes drop
a slow flowing tear
when you feel with the poor

Love peace and serenity
Love, live your dreams.

DREAMS WILL YOU CARRY ME

(قَدْ صَدَّقْتَ الرُّؤْيَا ۚ إِنَّا كَذَٰلِكَ نَجْزِي الْمُحْسِنِينَ - 37.105)

Dreams, will you carry me on your wings?
to fly with me to the land of freedom
into the land of everlasting light
where shadows don't exist.

Endless grace enters into my inner caverns
Grace embraces me in hope and joy

Look!
new memories take shape
in celestial light
as angels delight
to remain with me
to comfort my lone
suffering soul.

'When there ariseth in your midst a prophet, or a dreamer of a dream, and he hath given unto thee a sign or wonder." (Deuteronomy 13.1)

"You have fulfilled the vision." Indeed, We thus reward the doers of good." (Qur'an
(قَدْ صَدَّقْتَ الرُّؤْيَا ۚ إِنَّا كَذَٰلِكَ نَجْزِي الْمُحْسِنِينَ - 37.105)

TELL ME OF YOUR DREAMS

Come with me my love

Let us climb the rainbow
till we reach the top of the bow

Shall we sit there hanging our legs
and talk little things and laugh?

Tell me
of your dreams
my love

Tell me
of your anxieties
in love

Let me smile with you
being one with you
in your smile
and in your tears.

"And we dreamed a dream in one night, I and he; we dreamed each man according to the interpretation of his dream." (Genesis 41.11)

"It is a mixture of false dreams, and we are not learned in the interpretation of dreams." (Qur'an 12.44 - قَالُوا أَضْغَاثُ أَحْلَامٍ ۖ وَمَا نَحْنُ بِتَأْوِيلِ الْأَحْلَامِ بِعَالِمِينَ)

TWO PLANTAINS

Why do we multiply our possessions
and reduce our values?

Why do we love little
and hate too often?

We have learned to make a living,
but not a life.

Is it true my friend
that we have added
years to life
but not life to years?

WHY DO WE BUY MORE BUT ENJOY LESS?

I gave two plantains to a poor woman
on the lonely street begging
She took them with a great smile

There was light in her eyes, and I saw
she shared TWO plantains with her FOUR children.

She sat with tearful eyes
wiped the face of her children
and she smiled

It was the smile of God.

"For he has satisfied those who thirst, and those who hunger he has filled with food." (Psalm 107.9)

MAY I TOUCH YOUR LIFE

May I touch your life?

Like the dew drops touch
the tender leaves
on a beautiful dawn
I like to touch your life

I saw you
in all beautiful colours
in the garden
in the blossoms
in their vibrant nature

In the soft wings of butterflies
I saw you and my heart was overjoyed

I saw my angel walking and flying
flitting to and fro
with a happy heart
gentle, loving and kind

I heard your softest whisper
and felt your presence and love.

"Please come closer so I can touch you, my son. Are you really my son Esau or not?" (Genesis 27.21)

SWEET SECRET

I found a sweet secret
to tuck deep inside,
When you told me
my precious friend
that we shall be best buds
for now and evermore

I looked often around
to find my heart's yearning
No one can live alone in this world
friendship should come from
deep within the heart
Your wonderful friendship
means so much to me

For there's little that lasts
So much fades away.

Poet's Note :- This was published in Poet Freak under the name of Genova Maa. Genova was my beloved mother. She died at the young age of 38. I want to keep her name alive as long as I am alive.

Editor's Note :- The poet never had a physical mother named Genova. Both her parents were alive at the time of publication of this book.

"So David went to a secret place in the country: and when the new moon came, the king took his place at the feast." (Samuel 20.24)

LITTLE ANGEL STROLLED

Mellowed to that tender light
the little angel strolled in beauty
on starry skies
cloudless climes
on elysian fields
the realm of beauty

I felt the nameless grace on her face
softly lighten her little eyes
serene expression of delight
love and surprise

The angel of the Lord
took wings of a beautiful butterfly
came to her sweet dwelling place
serene, pure and full of grace

On that cheek
and over that brow
the angel kissed
It was goodness pure
peace and beauty
a heart so full
of innocent love.

"And I took the little book out of the angel's hand, and ate it up; and it was in my mouth sweet as honey: and as soon as I had eaten it, my belly was bitter."
(Revelations 10.10)

PART – V

LAMENTS OF HEART

CRYING OUT FOR OTHER HALF

THE TWO HALVES OF GOD

Two is joy. In creation everything is created in only two. Even the sprouting bud comes in twos. Sun and moon, day and night, two ears, two nostrils, two eyes, two cheers, two legs, two hands, two lungs, two hearts make one love. Two breasts for a single child. Two ovaries for a single uterus, two cheeks for a single face. And Two was God split into when he wanted to make Love

For ages I have been kept hungry and imprisoned in a cave. Now you are filling the parched deserted heart with heavenly ambrosia. Oh god, when divine energies flood in, what could mortal souls say. Now you are feeding this famished soul, whose intestine's capacity is just a hole of blue sky and a pinch of golden sun light. You are filling my whole with ocean of love when my heart's capacity is that of a newborn baby to suckle just a drop of its flavour.

I am every day morning brushing their teeth, oiling their hair, combing, powdering, milking them, feeding them, clothing them, caressing and fondling them, laugh with them, show them sky, birds, mongoose, owls, bats and all that my eyes could see, sing songs to them, kiss them with my loving heart. What not I do for them. Now when I open my heart and show to you, you say oh, it is only a shoe flower..."

TWO HEARTS

Two hearts yearn
for each other

The simple touch
holding hands together
the smile and the feeling
of being loved
without feeling
the flow of time

You feel the absence
of the loved one

Heart does not understand
that absence is only temporary.

The heart is yearning.
Love is a mystery.

....

When you sang
the notes turned into little hearts
They flew into the crimson skies

When i sang, the hearts that flew up
came back to you as butterflies.

"Draw nigh to God, and He will draw nigh to you; cleanse hands, ye sinners! and purify hearts, ye two-souled!" (James 4.8)

WHERE INNOCENT HEARTS MEET

Shining tears of my eyes
are my gifts today for you
loving thoughts
and listening ears
echoing soul
and caring hands
are my sweet gifts to you today.

I fly with untiring wings
to the land of songs
and wild butterflies
where innocent hearts meet
to love, and to love alone.

"We will be innocent if we carefully keep all these commandments before the Lord our God, just as he demands." (Deuteronomy 6.25)

KEEP ME IN YOUR HEART

Keep me in your heart safe
in my sufferings I will think
I am secure

Sing to me songs eternal
allow me to smile in grief
and in anguish

Tell me stories of love
give me a mouth kiss
that is tender

Keep me safe on your lap
sing me a lullaby
help me to dream
of a rebirth in heaven.

In my new awakening
i shall hear angels singing

They will then cover me
with the kindest embraces
of sweetest harmony.

"And he gave me teaching, saying to me, Keep my words in your heart; keep my rules so that you may have life." (Proverb 4.4)

MY CAPTURED HEART

I want to fly away but cannot
my heart has been captured
by 'The One' who is unknown

Like the lotus opening up its petals
at the first rays of the glorious sun
i stand before your holy altar

You are hauntingly familiar to me,
yet so distant and far and far awa.

Why do you play with me like this?
Don't you know my heart longs for you?

"You have captured my heart, my sister, my bride. You have captured my heart
with one glance of your eyes, with one jewel of your necklace." (Song of Solomon
4.9)

SANCTUARY OF MY HEART

I heard his steps
in the depth of the night

It slowly became rhythmic
I heard the songs of his dance

He danced
to the rhythms of my heart

I ran to see him
with burning desire

His music flowed through my veins
I heard his rhythmic steps
dancing around me in the joy of love

But my eyes failed to see him

I live now in those sweet memories
of his footsteps

I hear my heart
dancing to his tunes

My heart is now
a sanctuary of peace.

"Let them construct a sanctuary for me, so that I may dwell among them. As the
pattern of the tabernacle and the pattern of its furniture, so you shall construct it."
(Exodus 25.8-9)

GOD HEARS MY HEART

Purify me, O Lord
My life is an open book before you
Wash me more and more
every night and day
I cannot hide my sins from you
Touch and purify my heart.

My offering today
shall be my contrite heart
You will not cast away
a tearful contrite heart

Do not turn away from me
wash me in your mercy
and take me to you

I want to be in your presence
at dawn and dusk

I like to sit before you
and muse about your wonders

I delight in your plans for me.
when I know of it, your plans
my heart is full of joy
Who am I Lord that you think of me?

I know when I cannot pray in words,
God hears my heart.

CANVAS OF MY HEART

I painted in orange
and red colours
with fiery power of passion
your face on the canvas
of my heart.

In your ready warmth
you illuminated my being
always in unspoiled white
in serene purity
oh so gently
you kissed me into ecstasy

My rainy tears of joy
flew down silently
and washed me

Losing in your love
I found myself.

"My mouth shall speak of wisdom; and the meditation of my **heart** shall be of understanding." (Psalm 49.3)

COME TO ME O HEART'S SOLACE

Come to me, my heart's solace!

I want to hold your hand tight today
my heart just throbs loud
when I see your face in my mind

Why do roses in me shed fragrance
when you fill my thoughts?
Why do they brighten up
when I smile with you?

Utter into my ears
words of love
true and noble
fill me with love

I want to smile and sleep
and forget myself
until the new dawn.

"Create in me a clean **heart**, O God; and renew a right spirit within me." (Psalm 51.10)

HEART FLIES TO MOON

My heart soars free
and flies to the moon
for in moonshine i can pray

Naked I stand
in moonlight
and wait for him
to come to me unawares
and kiss my whole being
in my utter nakedness.

Oh how I long for love's touch
to pierce my inner soul.

"God made two great lights: the greater light to rule the day and the lesser light to rule the night. And He made the stars as well" (Genesis 1.16)

"And of His signs are the night and day and the sun and moon. Do not prostrate to the sun or to the moon, but prostate to Allah, who created them, if it should be Him that you worship." (Qur'an 41.37 - وَمِنْ آيَاتِهِ اللَّيْلُ وَالنَّهَارُ وَالشَّمْسُ وَالْقَمَرُ ۚ لَا تَسْجُدُوا لِلشَّمْسِ وَلَا لِلْقَمَرِ وَاسْجُدُوا لِلَّهِ الَّذِي خَلَقَهُنَّ إِنْ كُنْتُمْ إِيَّاهُ تَعْبُدُونَ)

FOR WHOM MY HEART BEATS

Come and lie on my lap my beloved
I shall caress you and comfort you
relieve yourself from stress
be calm and quiet.
bide awhile
sleep awhile on my cosy lap

I am yours
all yours

Under the flower tree
I sit with him on my lap
and play mellifluent melodies
on my little flute

I play and sing only for him
He is my lover
and my only one,
for whom my purple heart beats.

"My heart is fixed, O God, my heart is fixed: I will sing and give praise." (Psalm 57.7)

LIFT UP MY HEART

Play on your harp
my angel of love
my guardian angel

Come down from the white skies
to walk with me here on earth

Play on your harp
my angel of beauty
Fill my heart and soul
with mellifluous melodies

Lift up my heart
to the presence of God
so that i may be lost
in meditation of the goodness
and kindness of my eternal lover

Come, lift up my heart
O my beloved angel.

"My heart is sore pained within me: and the terrors of death are fallen upon me."
(Psalm 55.4)

FURNACE OF MY HEART

All my words shall merge
into the living Word of God.
it shall be purified in the fire of love
in the furnace of my heart

In the waiting womb of my soul
God's word shall fall
like seeds in pure stillness

It will germinate there
in a centering silence
like a pupa bringing forth
the colorful butterfly

Conceived in love,
the spirit shall flow
from heart to heart
with the nectar of love.

"For my days vanish like smoke, and my bones burn like a furnace." (Psalm 102.3)

LET YOUR HEART SING

Fill the world with your song
Forget your troubles

Let your heart sing

On golden wings fly high
to the world of your dreams

Throw down from the heights
all your dark and grey thoughts

As it falls catch it and sell it
to buy the morning rays

Then you will be happy
a whole life long

Happiness is your birthright
Be free like a flying bird
It is going to be a wonderful day.

"That my soul may sing praise to You, and not be silent.
O Lord my God, I will give thanks to You forever"
(Psalm 30.12)

FLAME IN YOUR HEART

Light a flame
in your heart

Let me see you
through the flame

Come to me through
the flame until
you and me burn.

"They with the imagination of their heart are like an oven, their sleep is all night like
the sleep of a baker, in the morning is he as hot as the flame of fire." (Hosea 7.6)

I WISH I COULD ENTER YOUR HEART

I wish
i could peep
into the blue deeps
and then find
what binds
them behind?

I wish
i could swim
along the clouds
and caress
those sky beds
and smell
what golden grace
fills them eternally fresh?

I wish
i could whisper
to the birds
in their codes
and lovely notes
and ask them
how they carry
the breeding theory
from nest to nest
with bubbling fest

I wish at last
that I could enter
the wonderful hearts
inside the starry looks.

TELEPATHY OF MAGIC HEARTS

Some magic heart types
I could hear the words
some magic lips mutter
I could taste the butter

somebody sings
I flutter with wings
some heart beats
mine reverberates feats

telepathy - thy name is sweet
a child of echo am I
mirroring your face of fictions
your looks of emotionless actions.

passions swim across the air
lust takes shape into a fair
questions quiz you in and out
sadness paints in you the oil canvasses.

face to face they are empty and alien
heart to heart they speak in volumes in train
empathy, sympathy, but not apathy
telepathic codes are heavenly swords.

"Then you will look and smile, you will be excited and your heart will swell with pride. For the riches of distant lands will belong to you and the wealth of nations will come to you." (Isaiah 60.5)

PART – IV

PAEANS OF LOVE

LOST IN THE OTHER SELF

LOVE ALONE

The whole life is a search for a little bit of love. If we do not get it, we become psychologically and physically ill. If we experience it, then there is Rhythm in our souls and we dance in those rhythms...

All the moments in which you do not love, are wasted moments of life which will never come back. Our call is to love. There is no meaning in life without love.

Love and love alone can bring you into the world of beauty. Your soul is in need of love. The deepest longing in you is love. Love is spiritual nourishment.

Love is God's hands and arms. He hugs his beings through love. When we are pure in mind, or when there is no mind, God puts his hand made of divine energy through our hearts. Through us that hand goes to the heart of our beloved. Now who are you, and who am I, to stop, start, punctuate, and intervene that love?

ARMS OF MY BELOVED

In my tearful dreams
I saw the path of light
Lead me to the abode of love
Let me sit and rest for a while

My lips longed for his kisses
I spoke of my deepest longings
And then I saw my beloved
Walking slowly to me like a fairy

In the ecstasy of that love
Joy tremendous filled my mind
I fell into the arms of my beloved
And my heart danced to his rhythms.

"In his love and in his pity he took up their cause, and he took them in his arms, caring for them all through the years." (Isaiah 63.9)

MY EAGER LIPS

It is for you I wait
alone, endlessly
before my own inner shrine
You promised you would come
I shall wait the whole night through
until morning rays fall on my hair
in sheets of gold

my wings flutter
my fingers flutter
my Spirit flutters
when I see you
with eyes of my soul

I have nothing to offer you,
only my waiting, eager lips.

"But I would strengthen you with my mouth, and the moving of my lips should
assuage your grief." (Job 16.5)

I YEARN FOR HER KISSES

In my childhood
I loved playing in the rain
I sang songs in the rain
My mom scolded me

But one day I took her
also with me in the rain
She began to sing with me
and danced in the rain
She hugged me in the rain
singing all the way

These are my sweet memories
of my childhood with beloved mom

Today I yearn for her kisses

I feel the delight
now in this moment of rains
when I drink all that passion

Close your eyes
see with your real eyes
my lips drinking her passion.

"Let him kiss me with the kisses of his mouth: for thy love is better than wine."
(Songs of Solomon 1.2)

BEING IN LOVE

When the romance
turns into commitment,
"Falling in love" is over
Being in love begins

Being in love
is a state of the soul
where lovers nurture
through surrender

Surrender
the needs of Ego
to the true needs of Spirit

Then emerges love
"True love"
as if from nowhere

That is the lovers' world,
the World of the Spirit.

"There is no fear in love: true love has no room for fear, because where fear is,
there is pain; and he who is not free from fear is not complete in love." (John
4.18)

LOVER OF MY HEART

The lover of my soul
took me to the rainbow
He painted my body all over
with shining colours of the rainbow.
Then he hugged me so intimately
looked into my eyes
and kissed me.

I love you
the owner of my heart
my unseen lover.

"Set me like a cylinder seal over your heart, like a signet on your arm. For love is as strong as death, passion is as unrelenting as Sheol. Its flames burst forth, it is a blazing flame." (Songs of Solomon 8.6)

DARING TO LOVE

I am not even a worm
not even an ant
not even a mustard seed

But I do dare to seek you,
do I dare to love you

In my fear I dare
in my passion I dare

But how do I dare
to love You?

Your love gives me the dare
beyond all worldly care

And this daring you give me
all day long and in the night

"Thou shalt love the Lord thy God with all thy heart, with all thy soul, with all thy strength, and with all thy understanding; and thy neighbour as thy self." (Luke 10.27)

STILL DARING TO LOVE

Can this heart be quiet?
Love lingers inside
like a flaming inferno

But afraid of the hurts

Still daring to love
still in silent hope
to meet the feathered queen
to touch her soft bed
of wild passion.

"Love has in it no element of fear; but perfect love drives away fear, because fear
involves pain, and if a man gives way to fear, there is something imperfect in his
love." (John 4.18)

LOVE THOUGHTS

May the flame of love glow in your heart
May your life be filled with love
Hope and peace.

May you be content with the little joys
Which life provides you every day
May God touch you in a very special way

Remember not the one who hurt you yesterday
But remember the one who loves you today

Let all the love experience be tender
Let it satisfy your body and soul

This is my wish for you today.

"So now, if you wish to show gracious love and truth toward my master, tell me so.
But if not, tell me, so that I may go elsewhere." (Genesis 24.49)

LOVE IS SACRED

Love is most sacred in its core
free from impurities of the world
so when you let someone too near
he or she becomes a part of you

In the sacred kinship of real love
two souls are deeply united
for there is no other, no alter
the two are one and the same

When you love, you open your life
to your lover breaking all your barriers

Your protective shell breaks
the person you love is given
absolute permission to enter
into the innermost temple
of your spirit making you feel

Love is most sacred in its core

"Though I have the gift of prophesying and know all sacred secrets, all knowledge, and all faith so as to move mountains, yet have not, love, I am, nothing." (Corinthians 13.2)

REAL LOVE OFFERING

Love that comes from the Almighty
has no ambition, envy or jealousy

This love is illuminative
and fills the whole being

Love combines every quality
that belongs to the higher Sphere

Birth of all that is noble and good
are from real and pure love

Beauty is born out of real love
humility is born out of real love
fineness and goodness
kindness and sympathy
are born out of real love
charity is born out of real love
all kinds of arts and music
are born from real love

When you offer your sincere love
you need not be afraid of anything

You draw the energy
of such a pure love
from indwelling Spirit of God

Always ask yourself:
"Am I sincere when I give my love?"

FLAME OF LOVE IS WAITING

We cannot fill up our emptiness
with objects, possessions and people

We have to go much deeper
deeper into that emptiness
to find beneath the nothingness
the flame of wild love waiting
to embrace and to warm us

to bruise us, guide us
to shear us, to free us
of our earthly shackles
we must find that love

In and through the warmth
and creativity of true love
soul shelters us
from the bleakness
of bare nothingness

For beneath that nothingness
Flame of love is waiting

"Put me like a seal on your heart
Like a seal on your arm
For love is as strong as death….
Its flashes are flashes of fire,
the very flame of the Lord!"

(Songs of Solomon 8.6)

131

LOVE EMANATES FROM LOVE

There is only one God
from whom alone emanates
all love and light in the world
God is wisdom and innocence

You are getting that light
and warmth from the sun
You enjoy it every day
But you can never become
a sun – such a sun yourself
however you may desire
You never become a sun.

Love is giving
in its nature
Love is sharing
by its nature
This sharing of love
spreads its light
in all directions
from your person
like rays of sun
when you begin to give

Unshared love
is no love at all.

"To you belongs gracious **love**, because you reward each person according to
what he does." (Psalm of David 62.12 – In Judea Wilderness)

LOVE COMES IN A MILLION VARIATIONS

Love is ardent,
burning, gentle

love is strength

It envelops you
all the mornings
and evenings
in soft layer of
feathery wellness

Love is soft
it raises you
to the heights
of sheer ecstasy

Love shoots its waves
in millions of variations
to distant horizons

Did you ever experience
such a heavenly love?

"Many waters cannot quench love, neither can the floods drown it. If a man gives all the substance of his house for love, it would utterly be condemned." (Songs of Solomon 8.7)

"Her many sins have been forgiven, because she did love much; but to whom little is forgiven, little he doth love.' (Luke 7.47)

FEAR OF LOVE

A child burns her hand
on the kitchen stove
and a fear of fire begins
in a tender moment
a hand is slapped
and a fear of love begins

emotional associations
and reflections run deep
beneath the surface
our heart breathes
like a soft sandy bottom
waiting under water

Still the currents
till you are transparent
like a calm winter lake
when it is still and clear
others can also see through
to our very inner bottom
and it will make love
possible again

So stay with your feelings
long, long, long enough
till the ripples settle.

"Love has no element of fear; perfect love drives away fear, because fear involves pain, and if a man gives way to fear, there is something imperfect in his love." (John 4.18)

SEEDS OF LOVE

I have seeds in my soul
It will burst into flowers
only in the rain of tears

I have seeds of love
in my ardent soul
It will fall into fruition
only in the raging fire
of burning intimacy

long summers of hope
have made me thirsty
with desire of new love

with coming of rain
I offer you my seeds
I am waiting for love

to fructify.

"The seed also of his servants shall inherit it: and they that love his name shall dwell therein." (Psalm 69.36)

"The Lord will circumcise thine heart, and the heart of thy seed, to love the Lord with all thine heart, and with all thy soul, that thou mayest live." (Deuteronomy 30.6)

REAL POET OF LOVE

A real poet has to be
a living expression
of the love of God
for a light bearer he shall be
being all things to all men
for the sake of Lord God.

Love is the only force
moving the universe
love is above all things
and is the sum total
of mystical thinking

True love alone helps a poet
to make sense of his own thoughts
and to coax, guide and direct others
in and through his lofty verses

A shoulder to cry one, arms to lean on
a mouth to cheer, a heart to bear
ecstasies and agonies of a million

that is exactly the vocation
of one who has found true love
this self-felt responsibility
makes the wandering poet
a torch bearer for humanity.

"My heart is stirred by a beautiful poem. I say – 'I have composed this special song
for the king; my tongue is as skilled as the stylus of an experienced scribe'." (Psalm
45.1)

BECAUSE YOU LOVE ME

Because you love me, God, I shall live
Because you love me, Lord
I want to live - for you and for others

Because you know me, God, I can trust you
Because you know me, God
I want to trust you more and more deeply

Because you call me, Lord, I can follow you.
Because you call me, Lord
I want to live with you – with you till eternity

You are the reason of my life
I thank you very much for it.

I can certainly find myself in you.

Poet's Note :- This prayer was given to a girl who wanted to commit suicide. She repeated this prayer very often and now she is a happy person.

"For this **reason** the Father loves Me, because I lay down My [own] **life** so that I may take it back." (John 10.17)

MOON BEAMS OF LOVE

Love beams of moon
of wondrous delight

spread on me, warm light
of magical exuberance
filling me with ardent love

Come, lift me tonight
to your heavenly abode

Cheerful, cute, bright, lively
and vivacious are my senses

Come, kiss my forehead
help me to my reverie

I spend my nights reclining
on moonbeams of love.

"The moon and stars shall rule the night, for his loyal love endures forever." (Psalm 136.9)

"The Hour has come near, and the moon has split in two." (Qur'an 54.1 - اقْتَرَبَتِ السَّاعَةُ وَانْشَقَّ الْقَمَرُ)

SONGS OF LOVE

Sing songs of Love
Lift your hands to Heaven
Set your heart to music
Sing songs of Love

The angels are playing
Their celestial Lyre
Do you hear it?

Sing songs of Love
Spread wings of flame
Set your heart aflame
Sing songs of Love

Listen, listen, listen
Close your eyelids
See in your mind
Angels flying around
With golden harps
Eager to play
Only for you.

"I will sing for my be**love**d my **love-song** concerning his vineyard: "The one I **love** had a vineyard on a very fertile hill." (Isaiah 5.1)

TRUE LOVE

it lends you smiles
when the world dies within
it lightens your sighs
when you sink sagging sideways

it is monsoon unexpected
raining in hot summer
when scorching sun glimmers
and dehydrates you drier

it is sweet to ugly
kind to penniless
it kneels down to the leper
and stands up to the tender

it sparkles in those looks
like stars from heavenly pegs
it sprays upon the scar
like a balming milky bar

it speaks in silence
soaked with resilience
when every leaf has dropped
it fans with a heart unstopped

"Your love must be true. You must always turn in horror from what is wrong, but keep on holding to what is right." (Romans 12.9)

LOVE MISSILES

Missiled
across globes
love reaches
earth's corners
from hearts unseen
hands pen
words spill
from memories sweet
sore, sad or simply funny
sharing thoughts
scenes, emotions, feelings
bridges of love built
by sites of goodness
electronic love
invisible to the eye
eyeing by reading
forming an image
from poems we read
a poetic image
electronic hands
digitally hugging
one another
with kiss icons
all computerized
and our future babies
they are all e-booked.

"Meditation is the bow, love is the arrow; Supreme God Brahman is its sole aim…" (Mundaka Upanishad 2.4)

SING A LOVE SONG

Would you sing to me
a love song now
I am all ears for you

Would you murmur in my ears
words of everlasting love
I am dying to hear you

The clouds rain down
on those alone who love
their singing hearts filled
with the warmth of love

Lift your mind, love
in ever watchful hope
God's grace will fill you

O come,
Sing to me now
Your songs of love

"You are to them like a love song by one who has a pleasant voice and plays well
on a stringed instrument - for they hear your words but do not practice them."
(Ezekiel 33.32)

CHASTITY IN LIFE AND LOVE

ah poor mind
embroiled in kinks
of a thousand kinds
of trifle little things
loses its chastity
ending up in vain
wasteful things

ah poor maid
not knowing how to meet
the gnawing poverty
and biting insecurity
relents to leasing
her youth and beauty
spending her energy
that costs her purity

ah milk adulterated
losing its bonding strength
separated and soured
invaded with germs galore
curd they call such milk spoilt
but having lost its fluidity
lovely milk has no more purity

on its way down the hills
flows the turgid river
mixed with sundry gravels
with its story of lost sanctity
purity going steadily downhill
could you blame rivulets for this

helpless the river
flows downhills

let us now catch
the wavering mind
the whistling wind
and tune the same
to a single sound
lest that too gets weeded
with seeds of filthy creeds
with mind singly focused
let us light our prayer lamps
let not the disturbed mind lie
at the feet of divinity high
but only noble feelings breed
let us not think of evil deeds
chaste is the mind clean and swept
of all intentions and hidden motives
just in innocence let the mind
in ever blissful joy abide.

"I will not punish your daughters when they become prostitutes. Or your brides when they commit adultery, for men themselves slip away with prostitutes, And they offer sacrifices with temple prostitutes. So people without understanding come to ruin." (Hosea 4.14)

"And those who accuse chaste women and then do not produce four witnesses – lash them with eighty lashes and do not accept from them testimony ever after. And those are the defiantly disobedient," (Qur'an 24.4 - وَالَّذِينَ يَرْمُونَ الْمُحْصَنَاتِ ثُمَّ لَمْ يَأْتُوا بِأَرْبَعَةِ شُهَدَاءَ فَاجْلِدُوهُمْ)

LOVE IS FAITHFULNESS

Love is truth
Truth is love

to be in love means
to be true to oneself
to love unconditionally
means you give yourself
with all your heart
and soul to one

and only to one

Love is when you realize
he/she is the best thing
that ever happened to you
and you want to cherish
that one very person
and the very moments
spent with him/her

till death do you part.

"I am like an olive tree flourishing in the house of God. I trust the loyal love of God forever and ever." (Psalm 52.8)

MAN WOMAN

Contemplate on sex
the sexual complementarity
of man and woman

Male and Female
Yang and Yin
X and Y
He and She

Plus and Minus
The chemistry
The geography
The physics
The biology
Of human love

Explore the nature
of marriage union
of love and lust
celibacy and virginity

Contemplate
On God's intention
Behind human love.

Poet's Note :- The Sexual Question - The why for every sexual question is found in this truth : God intentionally created our sexuality as a powerful metaphor for His covenant love. Everything God has created for us here on earth has a spiritual purpose. Our sexuality was intentionally created as a holy symbol or analogy reflecting how God loves us.

TWO PEOPLE ONE MIND

When two of you
are of same heart
and same mind

When you feel together
strive together, walk together
with the same intent

You feel greater potential
to stand firm, stay true
resist all the enemy
and maintain unity
of spirit and mind
and not fall prey
to an alternate philosophy
of unwholesome mindset

When God becomes
The Third Person
in such a partnership
your life will take on
ever new purpose
ever new meaning.

Poet's Note :- Reflections on the book of Ecclesiastes of the Old Testament of the
Holy Bible)

ROMANTIC RELATIONSHIP

Our romantic feelings
and sexual longings
should compel us not
just to have animal sex
but to pursue covenant

Of marriage and friendship
Of lifelong sharing, caring
Of soul companionship

We were created uniquely
for more than just a
sexual relationship

We were created grandly
for committed love
and intimate knowing.

"Mary said to the angel, "How will this be, since I am a virgin and have no intimacy
with any man?" (Luke 1.34)

MARRIAGE AS UNION

Marry not in haste
undertake the vow
of marriage union
reverently, seriously
and in constant fear

of the Lord

make it a binding affair
your marriage
an unbreakable pledge
before Lord God

where two human lives
are so knitted together
it is impossible tell apart
one part from the other

so united they are in love
that the fruitful fulfillment
of their hallowed union
becomes the heritage

and gift of children
for ages to come.

"'Then I passed by you and watched you, noticing that you had reached the age for love. I spread my cloak over you and covered your nakedness. I swore a solemn oath to you and entered into a marriage covenant with you, and you became mine." (Ezekiel 16.8)

LUST TRAP

Pornography
and masturbation
may seem harmless
but they are dangerous
and very destructive
for your union

They will mess you up
and destroy one day
your relationships

Stay away from lust
it is a clever trap
for eventually it will
cause your death.

Union with God
is much, much sweeter
than all your emotional
and sexual comforts

It is sweeter far
than all your dreams
than all your longings
and worldly illusions.

"Let not your heart turn aside to her ways; do not stray into her paths, for many a victim has she laid low, and all her slain are a mighty throng. Her house is the way to Sheol, going down to the chambers of death." (Book of Proverbs 7: 25-27 - Holy Bible).

MARRIAGE AND DIVORCE

Jesus also spoke of it
of the grave tragedy
of human divorce

it only started among Jews
during the times of Moses

"because of
the hardness
of men's hearts"
so they said

and disciples understood
from Christ's teachings :

that marriage was
a most sacred act
between a man
and a woman

which enter you should not
hastily
heedlessly
or unadvisedly

"The one bound to a wife should not seek divorce. The one released from a wife should not seek marriage." (Corinthians 7.27)

"It may be that if he divorces you, Lord will give him in exchange better wives than you : believing women, obedient women, penitent women, women who worship, women who fast, previously married women as well as virgins." (Qur'an 66:5)

ONE FLESH LOVE

Our breath is one, pulse is one
Our blood is one, passion is one
One is our thought, one our goal
One is our body, mind and soul

all scriptures
speak of it
glowingly
the one-flesh union
of marital sex

as against the infidelity
in quick promiscuous love
and the gross immorality
of stray sexual intimacy

true one flesh love
of a man and wife
in a human cross
is a picture of Christ
and his eternal union
with Church and God
and our call to be faithful
to our covenant with God.

"Therefore shall a man leave his father and his mother, and shall cleave unto his wife: and they shall be one flesh." (Genesis 2.24)

"All flesh is not the same flesh: but there is one flesh of men, and another flesh of beasts, and another flesh of birds, and another of fishes." (Corinthians 15.39)

LOVE OF A MARTYR

a flash of sword
a severed head
tumbling in pain
in thick blood red
but scribbling love songs
on enemy's dust laid
how man of god sang
even in his death bed

I read about the martyrs
who loved their God
more than their own lives

They offered themselves
to be persecuted till death
for their conviction and faith

I too will learn to believe
by following their lives
and their lofty deeds

I shall love my God
as they loved their god
till their last breath.

"If I donate all my possessions to feed poor people, and surrender my body to be burned, but do not have love for people, it is of no benefit to me." (Corinthians 13.3)

"Never think of those who have been killed in the cause of Allah as dead. Rather, they are alive with their Lord, receiving provision." (Qur'an 3.169)

GOOD NIGHT MY LOVE

Good night my love
I shall see you in my dreams

Like the lotus dancing in the presence of sun
Like the peacock dancing before his lady love
Like the lovebirds playing with their little beaks
Like the priest bowing and adoring
In front of his holy altar

Good night my love
I shall see you in my dreams.

May your sleep be like the colors of the rainbow
harmonizing together like a beautiful symphony

"Declare in the morning your loyal love, and your faithfulness in the night." (Psalm 92.2)

"Come, my love,
let's go to the field;
let's spend the night
among henna blossoms."
(Songs of Solomon 7.11)

"You cause night to enter the day, and You cause day to enter the night; and You bring the living out of dead, and You bring dead out of the living. And You give provision to people without account." (Qur'an 3.27 - تُولِجُ اللَّيْلَ فِي النَّهَارِ وَتُولِجُ النَّهَارَ فِي اللَّيْلِ

(وَتُخْرِجُ الْحَيَّ مِنَ الْمَيِّتِ وَتُخْرِجُ الْمَيِّتَ مِنَ الْحَيِّ وَتَرْزُقُ مَنْ تَشَاءُ بِغَيْرِ حِسَابٍ

PART – V

SOUL'S SONGS

ACROSS TIME AND SPACE

BE A CO-TRAVELER

Caught between the devil and the deep sea I am dying. Either I suffer from bereavement or drowned and soaked I get wet forever eternally drowned. What to do, I am too much in love that I am burning with love. O Lord, guide me to the other shore...

I have no secrecy in love. But a poet is the one who keeps plenty of secrets and sometimes spontaneously she begins to sing in her soul and then sometimes writes them down. When she forgets herself and writes her thoughts, it becomes a poem which touches and sometimes converts the reader. All love thoughts do not become poems. And I am no poet. I am only seeking your love. I am not seeking you, but your love alone....

Therefore do not first buy, but just be a co-traveler. In the roads of life, in the road to heaven, have a passer-by who shall forever be a companion, who needs no explanation for smiling or crying. Have a hand, that knows when to support, have a heart that knows when to throb, have a lip that knows when to kiss or not to. Have a hug that knows when to, or not to. Do not buy, but be a fellow good Samaritan. After all life is only a ladder to reach God's lofty paradise.....

SONGS OF MY SOUL

On the shoreless ocean
I heard the songs of my soul
sung by an unknown poet
harping a nameless tune

Her songs swell in melodies
in the depths of my being
and burst into wild flowers
of vivacious rhapsody
filling me with the fragrance
of the divine and eternal.

"The watchmen who make the rounds in the city found me, And I said, 'Have you seen him whom my soul loves?" (Song of Solomon 3.3)

TINY FLAME OF MY SOUL

The tiny flame inside my soul
is growing and growing
I feel its warmth and its flare
It is deep down in me
It is soft and steady

It is growing into flames
It is bright now and makes me powerful
It is my secret that I don't tell anyone

Meditate, sit and be silent
You can feel the flames in me
It will one day become a forest fire

The sparkle of dancing light in me
might burn you when you love me
Love is the quintessence of life
Without love, there is no life

"He makes winds his messengers, flames of fire his servants" (Psalms 104.4).

MY SOUL DANCED

I heard the angels at dawn
lost in rhythmic chanting
celestial tones of harmony
dancing with the tender rays
at the birth of a glorious morning.

My heart began dancing
My soul danced
My body danced
My spirit danced
with the holy rhythms
of angels of God.

Was it a mystical experience?

"Let them praise His name with dancing. Let them sing praises to Him with timbrel and lyre" (Psalms 150.3)

NEW BODY FOR OLD SOUL

Departed
the soul
is in search of
a new body
feelings
a new heart
fire
a new hearth
emotions
a new song
rain drops
a new mouth

every message sent
settles in a mind
reads the brain
spits the words
the essence paints images
and the subconscious
soaked with beauty
gives birth to impulses
every wind accompanies
a fragrance of life
every motion carries
the storm of passion
every day opens up
to newer dreams.

Death,
like a gentle blow to the petal
soft and fragile

aching to persist
yet, failing to exist
by the fabrics of breeze

mortals,
built of love and affection
of a copulated male and female lawn
half way up the marathon
the goals all set
down goes the chariot snapped
here, at this moment,
when death silently snatched
the unseen energy
a love embodiment soon designed
softly erasing the solid wordings
deleting life sperms are childish hands
no more, no more, no more
love lips tremble to utter
what is left behind
is an echo in the tunnel
just a bundle of 'if onlys'
just simply nothing
in the gay and gorgeous plumes
in the twitter of multi-toned music
emptiness, killing emptiness speaks
of agony and utter melancholy
choking life in the black holes.

"Just as men adorn themselves with new clothes by discarding the old torn ones,
similarly by discarding its old body, the soul seeks a new body" (Gita 2.22)

SOUL FRIEND

In the depth of our hearts
we yearn for a soul friend

In the love of a soul friend
we live as real persons
without masks or pretensions

all superficial lies
all functional untruths
and clever half-truths
of acquaintance fall away

You are as you really are
when understanding dawns
in experience of soul love

Understanding nourishes
your sense of belonging
when you are understood
you feel very much at home

once understanding comes
you at once feel free
and you release yourself
into the shelter cave
of the other's soul.

"A sweet friendship refreshes the soul" (Proverbs 27.9)

SOUL LOVE

Soul love reveals your
hidden intimacies of life

Share your innermost self
your mind, your heart
with your significant other
this alone will give you
your sense of belonging

soul has no limitation
of space, or time
there is no cage for soul
soul is a divine light
that flows into you
and into your Other

make such a bond
with soul love
that makes your friendship
indissoluble

No time nor space
can ever severe it
such a love will never
part even in death.

"Soul is her best friend, who has conquered her soul by her soul" (Gita 6.6)

WATER OF YOUR SOUL

Are your insides starting to shrivel?
God tells : Drink me then !!!

Internalize God. Ingest God in you
Welcome God into your inner chambers
and the outer workings of your life

Let God be the water of your soul

I need God's work, God's energy
God's lordship, and God's love

Make a prayer for the thirsty heart

God, i am thirsty, i want to drink from you
I can do all things through the Almighty
who gives me the needed energy and strength

I receive your love at this moment
in the form of thirst quenching water
be you my life's sole nourishment
nothing shall separate me from you.

"My soul thirsts for you, my body longs for you, in this dry and weary land where there is no water…." (Psalm 42.2)

"Standing in water I am thirsty; quench my thirst, Lord…" (Atharva 6.28.3)

THREAD OF MY SOUL

Run into my arms, love
call me by my name
oh dear my sweetness
in a voice full of tender passion

Bring me now
the thread of my soul
I had given you when
we began to make love
knit me now in my love
be the thread of my soul

Look !!!
the butterflies fly
the birds twitter
rainbows smile
when you lie in my soul
O maker of my soul

You are dear to me
forever and ever
till the end of times

You are linked to me
by the thread of my soul.

"As the spider moves along the thread it produces, so the soul dwells in the body
it creates…" (Mundaka Upanishad 1.1.7)

LIFT UP MY SOUL

A voice cries in the wilderness
"God is coming
prepare yourself
with humble prayers
and soul offerings"

Replenished with the food
of spiritual nourishment
I humbly beseech you
I want to be a part
of your divine mystery

Hold me firm to things of heaven
Protect me in your mercy
Lift my soul up to you

Fill my mouth with laughter
help my tongue to sing for joy

My heart is like a dry stream bed
send me rainbows and pouring rain

I carry sacks of seeds of sadness
Help me to return with joy in fullness

I have trusted you
I have set my hope in you
Do not leave me alone
Lift up my soul to you.

SOUL'S DIVINE HONEY

Love is soul's divine gift
will you come to me
to sip together
this divine honey
when the first rays
of this glorious dawn
break into the dew of
love, romance and harmony.

Soul is love's divine abode
will you assist me
in making together
this divine honey
when very first blooms
of this glorious love
usher in the dew
of love and harmony.

"The earth is honey for all beings, and all beings are honey for the earth...."
(Brihadaranyaka 2.5.1)

SOMEONE THINKS OF ME

Vibrations
of thoughts
they steal in
at silent nights
during day hours
somebody thinks of you
curses or loves
scorns or despises
some wave is on
it encircles your unborn

some messages
from the trees, birds
and unseen spirits
somebody sends you
signals to your brain
everything ingrained
y can you hear
what others can't hear
y can you speak to
persons whom you can't call dear

somehow, somebody, somewhere
forms the web with somebody
saving me from drowning further
saving me from sinking
into sucking gloom...

"One who departs from the world while remembering the original cosmic vibration,
shall reach the supreme goal...." (Gita 8.13)

SOUL MARRIAGE

In a spiritual marriage, the soul
or rather the spirit of the soul
or the divine spark
becomes one with God

Humility, intimacy, pure love
sharing, caring and great joy
ear to ear listening
eye to eye trust
heart to heart talk
chest to chest embrace
you find in a marriage of souls

God who is also Spirit
has desired to show
to certain noble souls
how far this love can go

Despite his infinite majesty
He condescends to unite
Himself so intimately
with the feeble creatures

In a spiritual marriage
soul dwells always in God.

MY SOUL MATE

A soulmate completes you
a soulmate inspires you
It is with joy of conviction
the soulmate loves you
no one forces him or her
the soulmate makes you
the person you wanted to be…

……………..

My soulmate
is on his way
he is so kind
gentle, honest
and funny

He makes me always
feel like a real queen
he is always down
for some adventures
he makes me always
feel warm safe in him

I know for a fact
he is on his way !!!

Poet's Note :- Living in imagination and hope to find the right soul mate.

Editor's Note :- When she met me, Hemangi Sharma told me that she finally found her soulmate, although it happened rather too late in her life.

PART – VI

PRAYER TALKS

THE JOYS OF MEDITATION

TALKING WITH GOD

God knows the thoughts of our hearts before they land on our tongues. One who tunes into God knows the thoughts welling up in all human hearts. One who loves God knows how to talk to God in silence.

For wherever life is, there is talking. Talking is a beauty of life link, of being in existence. Talk of feelings, talk of emotions, talk of not only words but heavenly responses to nature, wind, breeze, ocean, sky, birds and all. In silence body talks, in darkness inner light talks. At night the nocturnals talk. In peace hearts talk with love. In harmony music talks with symphonies. Talking without words is the most beautiful talking. Talking with dance, talking with lyrics, talking with memories, nostalgic. When you are old and alone, you will talk to photos of dead ones, to tombs of dead ones, to your beloved ones gone by. You talk to your own feelings, you talk to them who are in your consciousness. Talking is as enormous as your silent gifts of love.

Talk to God. Talk with your heart absorbed in God. Listen incessantly to God's silent talk. Do not underestimate the power of the Word. And do not forget that the pen is mightier than all the injustices that holy earth can contain. Writing is a source of personal soul-searching to find the meaning of life on earth.

PRAYER

God,
Seal my smile
With your sunshine
Cover me with
Tenderest of greens
Pour the pure oil of rose
On to my head
Kiss me on my forehead
Hug me so close
Until I forget myself.

Lord,
Give me your smile
Full of sunshine
Shower my love altar
With your lovely roses
Sprinkle your petals
On my prayerful breasts
Let me kiss your feet
With a song on my lips
Come, love me tonight
Until I lose myself.

"And when you pray, do not keep on babbling like pagans, for they think they will be heard because of their many words…" (Mathew 6.7)

MY PRAYER GIFT

It is my deep yearning
for you that I give you
as my prayer gift today
my God and my Lord.

As the deer pants
for the water brooks
so my soul pants
for You, O God.

(Psalm 42: 1 of the Holy Bible)

"Therefore I tell you, whatever you ask for in prayer, believe that you have received it, and it will be yours…" (Mark 11.14)

OIL OF GLADNESS

Fill me with the oil of gladness
that flows into my soul
from your divine chalice

In utter joy I present myself
before the immensity
and power of your majesty
thinking of your eternal
and universal kingdom,
a kingdom of truth and life,
a kingdom of holiness and grace
a kingdom of justice, love and peace

I like to sing a song
with Angels and Archangels
with thrones and dominions
with all the hosts and powers
praising you for evermore
until the end of times.

"Bestow on them a crown of beauty instead of ashes, the oil of gladness instead of mourning, and a garment of praise instead of a spirit of despair..." (Isaiah 61)

I BELONG TO YOU

I belonged to you
said the green leaf
to the tall Oak tree
and soon the wind blew
blissfully snatching the blade
from the cozy bed and fled.

I belonged to you
said the lovely drops to clouds
of bulging bags full of moisture buds
but then soon it rained
and poor drops fell upon the ground
sinking into sticky drains underground.

I belonged to you
said the newly married bride
to the loving husband new
as she laid her head rest
upon his fully grown chest
but fated days were born to test
and there he lied the handsome best
upon his cold grave married to dust.

I belonged to you, my God
said the heart pained and red
who knows what is due
the silent prayers stirring
hopes anew....

"So let no one boast in men. For all things belong to you… (1 Corinthians 3.21)

REAL LEADER

A real leader will never keep silence
He will raise his voice against all injustices
His desire to speak about goodness to all

When you raise your voice against evil
you take the risk of losing your life
but God's word is your strength
no one can shut the mouth up
of such an ardent believer of God

Give us all, your mighty words
that will encourage us
and keep us ready always
to fight against injustices

When worry and fear try to rule us
help us to shake it off from our shoulders
because we believe in the power of God
that is working in and through us

Give us your words of love
Give us your words of might.

"If a king judges the poor with truth, His throne will be established forever..."
(Proverbs 29.14)

IF YOU LIFT YOURSELF

If you lift yourself up to me
with all your heart and soul
I shall be with you in your hour of distress
for you have heard the words of my mouth

I shall clothe you with my robe of mercy
And gird you with my eternal joy
I shall fix you like a peg in a sure spot
I shall give you honor wherever you are

O Unseen God!
worshipping you in my secret temple
I offer you the incense of love
before your golden shrine

I shall sing your praises
playing on my veena

Would you be pleased
when I dance through night
in your holy presence
until the dawn breaks
into mild golden rays.

"Be strong and of good courage, do not fear nor be afraid of them; for the Lord your God, He is the One who goes with you. He will not leave you nor forsake you...." (Deuteronomy 31.6)

YOU ARE MY REFUGE

You are my refuge
my only refuge
would you send your angel
to preserve me in distress?

My heart listens to your murmurings
even in the depth of the night

Even when I fall sleep
you are always at my side

During the day I keep my God
ever in my sight, sensing
the fullness of His presence

You show me the path of life
I shall never falter and fall.

"Leave aside all other paths, and take refuge me in alone…." (Gita 18.66)

"God is our refuge and strength…" (Psalm 46.1)

GRAIN OF SAND

Inside an oyster shell
God plants a grain of sand
It becomes a natural pearl
so beautiful and so full of worth.

God planted you here on earth
so that you may grow and become
a pearl of beauty and great worth

A grain of sand is so insignificant
But God converts it into a pearl

However insignificant you may think
you are in the society around you
God can convert you into a person
of greatness and of great value

Work hard, study and pray
Unite yourself with Almighty
Do not work against the voice
of your own inner conscience
for it is in your conscience
where God lives and guides.

"If I count them, there are more than grains of sand; but when I finish the count, I
am still with you...." (Psalm 139.18)

BURN LIKE A CANDLE

You kindled me
You are very thoughtful
when you look at me now
You sit pensive in my light
and meditate

Do you know
I am glad I burn
If I did not burn
I would have been in a candle box
with others who also do not burn

In such a box
we find no meaning for our lives

My meaning I find when I burn
Now I'm kindled and spread light
You can say "I am on fire".
I am burning, a-burning
So I become shorter
I am sad, I will soon become
a small stump only

But so is life
I have two options only:
Either I remain completely
intact inside my cardboard
then I will not become smaller.
But then I have no meaning in life

Or I burn

But when I burn
I give light and warmth
and then only I will know
I am of use for others
I have given myself freely

It is better than to be as cold
and meaningless in the box

Burning for others is my joy.
A candle light is contagious
Be a candle that burns

Burns.

"No one after lighting a lamp covers it with a jar or puts it under a bed, but puts it
on a stand, so that those who enter may see the light…." (Luke 8.16)

BELIEVE IN GOD

Walt Disney was fired
from a newspaper
for lacking imagination
having no original ideas
Can you believe it?

Albert Einstein
unable to speak
until he was four years old
teachers said
he would never become
a success in life

Michael Jordan was out
from school basketball team
he went home, locked himself
in his room and cried

Steve Jobs, at 30 years old
was devastated and depressed
being unceremoniously removed
from the company he started
Can you believe it?

Work hard, believe in God
Believe in yourself foremost
You have great potentials
As a divine child of God
Do not think about what
Others think about you.

ACT A BIG SHOT

Act like a big shot
You are always admired
You are a somebody
Is it not seductive?

To sit always on the top
you are already up there
you can play with your influence
you can manipulate human beings
Is it not evil?

To act as a loving man
and play with others
with the sole intention
of lustful satisfaction
Is it not alluring?

And yet there was one
who refused to do so,
who lived so differently

Instead of profiting from power
He served the poor downtrodden
Instead of relationship games
He spread respect and trust
Instead of circling around oneself
He opened himself to God
He was Jesus of Nazareth.

STORM OF ARROWS

In God be the breath of all mankind
You are my breath when i pray to you

My flesh yearns for you
My soul sings for you
I carry your heart with me

in rain and in the sunshine
in snow and in hail storm
in darkest clouds and typhoons
in the shower of stones
and in the flurry of blows
your name is always with me

In the storm of arrows in the valley
i shall lift up my lowly heart
to you and shall not waver and fear

You are with me always, O my Lord.

"And His arrow will go forth like lightning; and Lord God will blow the trumpet, and will march in the storm winds of the south…." (Psalm 64:3)

MY PRAYERFUL WISH

I hold on to the search for my truth
to the perfect fulfillment of my dreams
and to the certainty of my surrender
in complete ascension towards Light

It is my faith I will succeed
in every aspect of my life

I have faith I shall overcome my fears
I shall thus receive what is best for me
I believe in everything that shines in me

I am creative, I am alive
I do not get stuck in routine
I put all dead habits aside
I open myself to experiences new

Every new day is different for me
Life's energies flow through me

I believe in everything
that shines in me.

"Therefore I tell you, whatever you ask for in prayer, believe that you have received it, and it will be yours…." (Mark 11:24)

MIND BREATH

breathe in fire, breath out ice
breathe in ice, breathe out fire

when we breathe in
we can feel the life force
entering into every cell
bringing us to restful peace

when we breathe out
we feel how our tiredness
weakness, fear and anger
slowly escape from body

thus with emotions neutralised
our disturbed mind sits in peace

a poetic mind needs this peace.

Poet's Note :- Breathing Slow - Some people react to anxious situations by breathing faster, which can worsen stress and anxiety. Consciously slowing the breathing down can control anxiety. Capnometry assisted respiratory training is a type of breathing therapy that promotes slow, mindful breathing. The participants perform breathing exercises twice a day. Panic disorder is different than anxiety, but the conditions share some symptoms.

"By neutralising the inward breath by outward breath, and likewise neutralising the outward by the inward, the wise attain tranquility….." (Gita 4.29)

PRAYER INCENSE

My prayer to Lord
is a sweet aroma
ascending slowly
to the face of God

My prayer pours out
my deepest thoughts
and all desires of heart
in presence of a loving God

warmth of his love
melts my heart
and enters my spirit
making my prayers
ascend to God
like the incense I offer
on his holy altar

In the holiest of holies
resides Lord God
aroma of my endless prayers
shall reach his sacred presence
soaking my penitent soul
that flies daily to Lord.

"Let my prayer be counted as incense before you, and the lifting up of my hands
as the evening sacrifice…." (Psalm 142.2)

CONTROL YOUR THOUGHTS

When a single thought
or a string of thoughts
keep repeating inside you
and if it is a sad thought
or a dark thought
it can lead you
to mental sickness

Pray in deep faith
it will help you conquer
all dark negative thoughts
repeating inside your mind
disturbing your mental peace

Offer all your thoughts
to God Almighty
and ask for the grace
to conquer it knowingly
and decisively

If in deep firm faith
you ask and pray
you will become free
from all ruminating thoughts.

"Just as elephants, lions and tigers are gradually controlled, similarly you can control your thoughts by steady practice...."" (Hatha Yoga Pradeepika)

PRAYER WALK

At least once a week
I may want to spend
some time strolling
on a prayer walk
through the woods

On a regular basis
I shall need to go
outside my comfort
on long prayer walks
if only to make sure
I am continuing on the path

Perhaps
I will need to study more
listen to more teachings
or order more books
On health and healing

Silence will take me
to my innermost core
where I can rediscover
myself ever, ever anew.

"For we walk by faith, not by sight…." (2 Corinthians 5.7)
"Do two walk together, unless they have agreed to meet?" (Amos 3.3)

MEDITATION

Sit comfortably in a place
free of distraction.

Focus on any doubts or worries
you might have about meditation.

Be completely open to your doubts.
Do not censor any doubt.
Examine each carefully.

Is it absurd?
is it valid or true?

Most doubts will be unmasked
spontaneously as absurd.

Consciously let go
of each doubt,
one by one.

Imagine it as a balloon
that sails away.

Let it vanish out of sight.

Poet's Note :- It takes time to master meditation, but it can be a helpful tool for managing anxiety. A single meditation session significantly reduced anxiety levels, as well as decreasing the physical stress on the arteries.

FLOATING

Very vivid shapes
and colors appear
within me and without
as well as this feeling
of floating on air

I flow out of my window
like a feathered bird
on a cushion of light
at the dead of night

by morning I am back
on my bed of dreams
pulled by the strings
of celestial light

I thank the world
for the threads of light
linking soul to soul
shared by all people
whose hearts are filled
with such innocent love.

Poet's Note :- Imagery - When you feel anxious about a situation or task ahead, guided imagery can help. This involves imagining completing the task that is causing anxiety calmly and successfully.

For instance, imagining finishing an important meeting or event before it happens can reduce anxiety about it. Some people also find it beneficial to visualize an environment in which they feel safe and relaxed.

MIND FRAGRANCE

If my mind has fragrance
i shall find you in that fragrance
I shall sense you and hug your smell
I shall breathe in your fragrance
that will penetrate my cells

My cells shall then bring me into prayer
and make me fall in adoration

When I breathe your fragrance
Your breath becomes my breath
Your mind becomes my mind
Your heart becomes my heart
By inhaling your very breath
I draw your soul inside me

Poet's Note :- Universal Mind - Is there an infinite storehouse of Ideas, knowledge, and power?

Editor's Note :- Many great thinkers of all ages have believed that man's stored information is not limited to his own memories of past experiences, and learned facts. There is one mind common to all individual men. It is the universal mind.

STILL SMALL VOICE

In my distress I cried
to my God for help

God listened to the still,
small voice from within

My cup overflowed
with the unmerited favour
of God's goodness

He raised me
from my brokenness.

"After the wind came earthquake, but the Lord was not in the earthquake; and after
the earthquake came fire, but the LORD was not in the fire; and after the fire there
was a still small voice. (1 King 19.12)

ADVAITA MUKTI

Not this, not that
Neither both these
Nor absence of both
What remains then
Is That

Advaita Vedantins
the Mayavaadis
see world as illusion
and seek moksha
spiritual liberation
by acquiring vidyā
or real knowledge
of one's true identity
as Atman, the Soul
and its oneness
with Spirit, Brahman

Advaita Vedanta says
Jivan Mukti
liberation in life
freedom from cycles
of birth and death
you can achieve in this life
in contrast to philosophies
that preach Videha Mukti
or moksha after death.

Editor's Note :- Advaita mean non-dualism or absence of the "other" – signifying
that God alone is real, all else being illusion.

VEDARITA

seek the eternal truths
of life and death
of the world beyond
whence you came
and where you go

covet not, give
fight not, forgive

who wrote them first
no one knows now
the hymns of Veda
the chants of Sama
they are eternally sung
by the lovers of God

Brahma Sutra to Vedanta Sutras
Bhagavad Gita to Upanishads
Sankara, Vyasa to Vadarayana
The sages of India have sung
the eternal glory of Brahman.

Poet's Note :- In the Vedic religion, Ṛta (/ˈrɪtə/; Sanskrit ऋत ṛta "order, rule; truth")
is the principle of natural order which regulates and coordinates the operation of
the universe and everything within it. Vedas describe Ṛta as that which is ultimately
responsible for the proper functioning of the natural, moral and sacrificial orders. It
is closely allied to the injunctions and ordinances thought to uphold it, collectively
referred to as Dharma. Vedic ṛtá and its Avestan equivalent aša are both thought
by some to derive from Proto-Indo-Iranian *Hṛtás "truth" which is similar to Veritas.

BUDDHA MUDRA

In all images of Buddha
the palms are folded
in one of the formalized
mudra positions

In Bhumisparsha Mudra
Buddha is depicted
in a seated position
the right hand resting
on the knee and fingers
pointing towards the earth

Left hand rests on the lap
with palm facing upwards
one hand giving benediction
other hand seeking union

Man, God, Earth, Saviour
Each one a link for other
Thus become chain connected
In the enlightenment of Buddha

Poet's Note :- The Buddha-to-be was meditating under a Bodhi tree when Mara the demon arrived accompanied by his armies and his three beautiful daughters. Mara's armies attacked the Buddha while his attractive young daughters tried to seduce him. The Buddha-to-be touched the Earth with his right hand, calling upon Mother Earth to be his witness. Earth Goddess Phra Mae Thorani appeared in the shape of a young, beautiful woman. By wringing the waters out of her long hair she drowned the armies of Mara, allowing the Buddha to continue meditating and reaching enlightenment. Bhumi Sparsha means "touching the earth" – or calling earth to witness.

EAST AND WEST

When will that day come
When poets alone will rule
And not bigoted dictators
Will that day come, Lord?

All our thoughts and insights
drawn from Asian wisdom
Buddhism, Taoism, Tantra
Zen, Jainism and Hinduism
Tanakh, Talmud and Granth
Avesta, Tipitaka, Agamas
along with New Testament
and thoughts of Jesus Christ
the eternal truths of Qur'an
when will they lead us
through intellect of nations
into a new world vision

poetic minds still dream
of east meeting the west
and this is a grand vision
which the modern world
badly needs today.

Editor's Note :- All my discussions with Hemangi Sharma were centred around bringing forth the underlying unity of all world religions and scriptures like Veda, Bible, Gita and Qur'an into a single comprehensive whole.

"Those in the west are appalled at his fate, and those in the east are seized with horror..." (Job 18.20)
"Not from east, nor from west, nor from desert comes exaltation..." (Psalm 75.6)

PRAYER BLESSINGS

Unexpected blessings
are coming on your way
because you were praying
when the whole world slept

Unseen powers above
are working overtime
in your favour now

God gives his ear
to your every prayer

Yours prayers are heard
now unexpected will be
your blessings in plenty

"Blessed is the man who trusts in the Lord, whose trust is the Lord..." (Jeremiah 17.7)

Give, and it will be given to you. Good measure, pressed down, shaken together, running over, will be put into your lap. For with the measure you use it will be measured back to you...." (Luke 6.38)

MIRACLE IN YOUR LIFE

There is always a place
for a miracle
in your life

Do you believe it?

Put all your heart
in whatever you do
think not of the fruits
but your actions

Capture the beauty
of every moment
and live fully in joy

Then you will wonder
at the miracle
that 'you' are.

"Unless you see signs and wonders you will not believe." (John 4.48)
"Everything is possible for one who believes." (Mark 9.23)

"With man this is impossible, but not with God; all things are possible with God."
(Mark 10.27)

PART – VII

SONGS OF SILENCE

PROMISES OF ETERNITY

SILENCE OF THE MONK

The monk was drawing water from a well with a bucket. A group of young men came and asked him :- Why do you waste your life living alone in silence?.

Peacefully the monk answered : Look at the water in the well. Now tell me what you see.

They answered : Nothing. The water is not peaceful at all.

After sometime the monk asked: Now you look in the well and tell me what you see.

They answered : We see our faces.

Look, when the water is peaceful, you can see yourself. So is with meditation in silence. You see yourself.

After sometime the monk asked again : Look and tell me what you see in the well.

They said : We can see clearly pebbles and stones at the bottom of the well.

So also is with meditation in silence.

You see everything in depth.

IN THE ISLAND OF TRANQUILITY

Relax and be at rest
Breathe again, breathe easy

Unwind, come to peace
find yourself, come to God

In the silent moments
gather your strength
in the island of tranquility

Let us renew our lives
in the depths of silence
God speaks at times
but in silence first
to our listening hearts

He created us in joyful silence
to live in loving companionship
together with him in heaven
to find his high abode of silence
is the divine duty ordained for us

And for that reason alone
our heart shall not be at rest
though our mind be silent
till it finds peace and joy
in Him the only Creator

"

Lord will fight for you, and you have only to be silent." (Exodus 14:14)

I REMAINED IN SILENCE

Today she came to me
She asked me to be silent

I entered my room
Did n't shut the door
Sat on my chair
Closed my eyes
Remained in silence

Time passed by
but i did not feel

She came
I heard her feathery steps
Felt her breath
Smelled her skin
She bowed I knew
Kissed me on my silent lips

I remained in silence.

"For God alone, my soul waits in silence…" (Psalm 62.1)

UNSPOKEN WORDS

The unspoken words
They wielded the swords
They touched the heart
With hands of firmest parts

Between the sounds
Of syllable mounts
When the intervals began
When music ended,
When the decibels nulled

In the magic clasp of fullness
I learnt the meaning
Of unsaid hearings
The unspoken words
Spoke of living images

In the gap
Like the hips of gentle laps
Consuming the ocean of seconds
The silence filled in
Creeping with invisible gleam
The unsaid words stroked my heart
With untold comfort, I stretched my feet

Unspoken beauties
Untouched realities
All left unadulterated
By the taste of sundry pirated.

INNER SPACE

The womb of God
welcomes me to dance
in feathery footsteps
to the play of universe
in pure silence

I experience at once
the intense vibrancy
and sensation of peace

invisible energies
come rushing in
and through my being

My inner space
explodes
in light.

"Be still and know that I am God..." (Psalm 46.10)

THE SILENT DESERT

Walk into the silent desert
Pray in the depth of the night

In the darkness of the desert
sink yourself into nothingness

Sit alone until you see the light
in your soul filling you with joy.

"Be still before the Lord and wait..." (Psalm 37.7)

"Worship of idols made of stones, metal, clay or jewels causes a man to undergo
repeated births. Therefore a seeker shall worship only within his heart; to avoid
rebirth he should shn outward worship..." (Maiterya Upanishad 2.3.17)

HEARING SILENT WHISPERS

Could you listen
to the voice
of somebody
when he thinks of you
from places afar
and feel his grief
or bear his agony
or enjoy his
lustful ironies

Could you hear
message of a being
carved in stone
or caged in nature's bone
as it releases
its records of ages
steaming with energy
or streaming along
with enormity

Could you feel
when you walk by
the side of a tree
shrouded in leaves
or sea or singing birds
or a stream of clouds
or in silvery nights
from the heart of nature
some secret code's key word
being uttered by its vibrations

Sitting in golden silence
when thoughts are imprisoned
by the breath of uniformity
as you go deeper and deeper
into the space of mind energies
the whole globe of oscillations
erupt as thoughts or messages
adsorbed in your externals, unaware
your mind swells in inner wisdom
and remains silent with mellowed truths.

"A time to keep silence and a time to speak." Ecclesiastes 3:7

"When the Holy Word is recited, listen to it and be silent, so that you may be blessed…." (Al Aráf 7.204 - Holy Qu'ran)

I HEARD THE THUNDER

Too early it was
when earth under sun
hot and humming
came the rains
cool and cajoling

Caught unbalanced
ponds danced up
air moistened
lipped them wet
the dry cups of noon lives

As I heard the distant thunder
my heart raced with teen age reminders
every time the noon rain comes
I feel aching pains within my brain
some distant dead one calls me hard
I feel the nostalgic throngs of long lost funs.

Editor's Note :- In deep meditation the cosmic vibrations are heard within the inner ears as sounds of distant thunders.

"Do you have an arm like God, can you thunder with a voice like His? (Job 40.9)

"Like a rainstorm from the sky within which is darkness, thunder and lightning. They put their fingers in their ears against the thunderclaps in dread of death. But Allah is encompassing…. (Quran 2.19) أَوْ كَصَيِّبٍ مِنَ السَّمَاءِ فِيهِ ظُلُمَاتٌ وَرَعْدٌ وَبَرْق

GUITAR NOTES ON OCEAN OF LIFE

As ego dresses fall one by one
you shiver in innocence revealed
candour and simplicity clasp you hard
your heart is filled with solemnity broad

When thoughts falter not astray by chaotic desires
ambitions climb not to monkey peaks maddening
and when you realise the path to wholeness
it lies when you beggar be, prides dissolved
beg for nothing but essential truths benign
just for melting beauty of creation, simple and childlike

when the inner being jewels and radiates through eyes
when the things you see don't matter but just pass by
when the objects you possess don't possess your mind
when you vibrate with nature and melodies infiltrate your mind
purity's guitar notes produce and you drown in Ocean of life.

Editor's Note :- Hemangi Sharma wrote and uploaded this poem on July 26, 2015 – just the day before she met me in person for the first time in this life. On the night of 26th she had spoken to me at length over phone.

WHISPER LAST NIGHT

What did you whisper last night?

The joy of your whispers
still lingers in my soul
at this glorious dawn

I forgot what you whispered
but the joy remains

Listen! the robins twitter
It is their whisper
In love they chatter.

Wake up to the beauty
of nature's gifts

Sense the wonders
and be keen in prayer.

"He hushed the storm to a gentle whisper,So that the waves of the sea were still…."
(Psalm 107.29)

INNER VOICE

There is a voice within
which no one
not even you
have ever heard

That voice is deep and firm
resounding with the truth
you have lived through life

When you speak from that deep inner voice
You are speaking from your unique
inner tabernacle of your own presence

Sense the beauty of this inner voice
Sense the power of your own truth

Poet's Note :- I published this poem in Micropoet under the name of my beloved
mother Genova Maaa who passed away at a young age. I published for a long
time with this second name.

Editor's Note :- The poet never had any physical mother named Genova. Both her
parents were alive at the time of this book's publication.

"Behold, You desire truth in the innermost being, and in the hidden part You will
make me know wisdom…" (Psalm 51.6)

"Therefore do not lose heart, for though our outer man is decaying, yet our inner
man is being renewed day by day…." (2 Corinthians 4.16)

IN THE SECRET CAVE

If you don't hear Him
in the secret cave of your heart
then your soul will cry

You should know
that in the innermost folds
of heart there is a voice
speaking to you always

This voice is not created
by anything that is corporal

You should enter
the inner caverns
of your being
in peace and quiet
in the bolted space

Then, close your eyes
Sit and listen

It is joyful peace

The cool breeze
of being with God
will caress your face.

"Men will go into caves of the rocks and into holes of the ground - before the terror
of the Lord, and the splendor of His majesty..." (Isaiah 2.19)

SWEET TRANQUILITY COME

Sweet tranquility, come
fill my breast and my breath
sink me in your light of love

Lead me from darkness to light

Light is knowledge
Light is wisdom
Light is holiness

Lead me O Light
from death to immortality

When God danced the dance of creation
light was born from nothingness
destroying darkness

Eternal God, give me this light
Let this universe awake in your light.

"While I am in the world, I am the light of the world..." (John 9.5)
""Lord, keep my lamp burning; God turn my darkness into light…." (Psalm 18.28)

SING IN THE SECRET CAVES

God chooses
many poets
from this world
to go out
and sing poems
of love and purity
in the secret caverns
of the human soul

Change human beings
Change human destinies
O Poets

Change hate to love
Change indifference to mercy
O Poets

Change death to immortality
Bring nectar from heaven to earth
O Poets

Be the mouth of Lord God
To sing in the secret caves
O Poets

God calls you
to sing his hymns
in this terrible world.

TOUCHED BY SILENCE

When I was touched
by his Silence
my eyes welled up

if only he spoke
I could stop crying
but his emotion overwhelmed

the tenderness flowed
down my whole being
as if I were a beggar maid
with nothing clothed
but his softness

I was moved beyond control
my body started vibrating
quivering my lips
but could not utter
a word of thanks
silently I watched
nobility pouring out
with no noise
no pretense

nor disturbing languages.

"There is one alone without a second. This knowledge is true solitude – not a
cloister, nor cave, nor a forest's depth…." (Maitreya Upanishad 2.3.6)

KISS OF SILENCE

On the banks of Ganges
I sit in a serene and sombre mood
Looking at the playful water
As the wind like a great artist
Draws playful lines
And circles on water

The wind tickles the water
And it laughs
Although I can't hear
When the water laughs
And jumps, it moves
In lines and circles
And then rushes swift to the shore

I sit there at the shore
With my feet in the water
And watch the lines and circles
Reach and kiss my feet
In reverent love

The wind is playful today
And comes to my lips
With a cold feathery kiss.

Editor's Note :- The poem describes the modifications of the mind stuff (Chitta Vritti). Water is the consciousness and winds the thought desires. The kiss at the end of the poem is the reward for perseverance in silent joyful meditation.

"My heart became secretly enticed, and my hand threw a kiss from my mouth…."
(Job 31.27)

PART – VIII

HYMNS OF GOD

PROMISES OF ETERNITY

HOUSE OF MY BELOVED

Whatever you give, you receive in thousand folds. If you give with a pure heart and a pure mind with pure intentions, when you are sharing your love, your whole being will be flooded with that Love.

Now I know, when I met you, that there is this god whom I had prayed all these days. See, with meeting you the whole thing is over. Now living is the plum of cake. You are asking will I eat the cake or not. See, if I eat it will be finished. So I will only lick and keep on licking so that the cake is okay. I can have the cake and lick the cake.

I want to go to my Beloved's house and die there itself, never to come back again. But when you go to the moon, you will realise that moon is like earth only.....

Love is not mine, neither yours, you cannot possess it, nor can you dispossess it. Every pure mind is permeable to love that flows through it. Like water that runs across when there are no dams, like rivers that flow through forests and wilds, love just flows through hearts when there is no barrier.

HAND OF GOD

You rich children of the world
you eat chocolates a mouthful
and throw away when you have your fill

You rich people of this world
you drink alcohol and vomit

You rich, you throw away meat
and it all lands in the waste bin

Here i am, begging for a piece of bread
a handful of rice, a glass full of water
The same God who created you
created me too

Shall i have a life to live
Shall i have a bread to eat

God has no hands to give
Your hands are God's hands

Ohhh rich of the world
would you hear my cry?

"For I was hungry, and you gave Me something to eat; I was thirsty, and you gave Me something to drink; I was a stranger, and you invited Me in…" (Mathew 25.35)

GOD IS WATCHING

The sinner hugs wrath and anger tight
Does not know how it destroys him
The vengeful will have no peace

Forgive injustice of your friend
Pray for those who offend you
In eternal anger if you live
Can God ever forgive you?

Forgiveness will liberate you
Your soul shall attain peace
It will remove fear from mind
Fearless you shall attain power

Forgive then your foes
Remember your last days
Set all enmity aside
Remember death and decay
Cease from sin
Overlook faults
Do not hate
Remember
God is watching you.

"He has forgiveness for all your sins; he takes away all your diseases…" (Psalm
103.3)

GOD SPILLS THEM OUT

Expressions are God's
he spills them out
forgetting his truths
eyes do not see
it is vision that catches the beauty
ears don't listen
it is audibility that signals match
tongues don't taste
buds have abstract nouns sleeping awake
sniffing fragrance
oh, it's not you, not you
it's the soul of smell seated inside the being
that divines the scent of reproduction
what is in a physical touch
any rubbing is not intimacy rich
It is the beauty of the inner soul
its purity that makes touches of bodies
melt into ecstasy immortal
sense organs are fake, they die
senses are born
sense organs perish
sensibilities rich
the little brained flatters self
carried by flashy eyes and ears
jutting out mortal ads
back, back, back more
from sense organs to senses
sensibly carried to reality
when the body evaporates its being
the being sings away, body stinks sinking.

Eyes don't see, visibility sees
ears don't hear, hearing is Abstract Noun
love is not touching, but an inner aching
of the inner souls seeking cohesive unity
expressions are neither yours nor mine
they uncurl like bountiful locks
like brooks that burst open
from the amazing wilds
spontaneous
they eject from the virgin minds
pure, fertile, untainted by painted egos
the minds, free and green, full of plenty love
energetic, unexhausted, they spill out
genius are gene born,
brilliance - brain's lightning
beautiful images tumble down
eternal beauties sketched and skilled
All expressions are Creator God's
modest, they gleam pure pearls.

"Yet the LORD hath not given you an heart to perceive, and eyes to see, and ears to hear, unto this day...." (Deuteronomy 29.4)

"And the eyes of them that see shall not be dim, and the ears of them that hear shall hearken...." (Isaiah 32.3)

EVER NEAR GOD

Even when I do not see you
Or hear you
You are ever near

When you live beyond the mountains
when you are above the flying skies
even when you dive deep
into the seas and remain
on the coral bed of ocean
you think of me always

From the silent skies you watch me
From the deep forests you hear me
With the passing breeze you touch me

I write love poems to you
as if you are a human being.

"Nearness of God to me is good, I have placed in the Lord my refuge….." (Psalm 73.2)

FIRST HOUR TO GOD

Dr. Martin Luther King, Jr
a journalist once asked him
how he found the time
to do all the things
he accomplished
in the course of the day

"When I get up
in the morning"
replied Dr. King
"I give first hour to God
And God gives me
all the rest".

So said the King

"Do this now, knowing this is a critical time. It is already the hour for you to awaken from your sleep…" (Romans 13.11)

"The sun of consciousness is ever shining bright; it neither sets nor rises. How can we perform then twilight worship?" (Maitareya Upanishad 2.3.5)

JOURNEY TO GOD

Only when journey to God is completed
begins the 'Journey in God'.

This is the essence of Eternal Life
It can have no end, no end
God is beginningless, endless

None who attained the End
ever came back to describe
their adventurous journey

And so no one knows
the length of the way
and the intense beauty
of experiencing that journey
in the Almighty God

For sure it is a journey
of eternity
in beauty
in light
in peace
in love.

"Then Jacob went on his journey, and came into the land of the people of the east…" (Genesis 29.1)

FRIENDSHIP OF GOD

Make me know your ways
Teach me all your paths
Help me walk in your truth
Always show the right path
To those who go astray

Your faithfulness
and love shall I praise
Your magnanimity
and grace shall I praise
I revere you my Lord
Your friendship is like breath
I cannot live without
your loving presence

Day and night I yearn
for your friendship Lord
Come to me
my Lord
come to me.

"His friendship is with them that fear him; and he will show them his covenant...."
(Psalm 25.14)

HAVE SECRECY WITH GOD

Unknown to other
men and women
you do so many things
that no one else knows

There are deeds you can do
which are known only to God
such deeds give tremendous joy
to a man or a woman in love

That is the secrecy of your heart
a secrecy between you and your God
you get the feeling that God is in you
ever watching you, protecting you

Have a secret chamber in your heart
Reserved for yourself and your love
Make love with him secretly, daily
No one else shall know your love
Such love moments are wonderful.

"Make haste my love, my dove, in the holes of the rock and in secret caves. Show me your face and let me hear your voice - for your voice is sweet and your romance beautiful...." (Songs of Solomon 2.14)

ENERGY OF GOD

Sun is a symbol
of God's energy

Add the energy
released by sun
plus the sum
of the energy released
by all the other stars
in the firmament
concentrated together

Multiply that energy
by infinity
then transpose it
into love
into pure unadulterated loving

This is the loving
that bonded God The Father
to all the human beings
from all eternity
to draw us back into God
who first conceived us.

Poet's Note :- Sun is a symbol for God's energy. Like most symbols they are no more than a shadow of the reality that they symbolize.

"The sun is still high. It's not yet time for the flocks to be gathered. Let us water the sheep, then let them graze…." (Genesis 29.7)

GOODNESS OF GOD

Glorify God with me this morning
Look towards God and be radiant

The angels of God are encamped
around those who revere the Almighty

Sit down in prayer and meditation.
lift your hands up to God
taste the goodness of His presence

Find refuge in Him in the real sense.

"Goodness and mercy shall follow me all days of my life; I shall dwell in the house
of the Lord forever...." (Psalm 23.6)

DANCING GOD

It is dance. Five mudras
Dance again. Three

The dancing God

Embraces,
penetrates the Mother

They are one motion
one silence

They are Word
Utterance and Return.

"Those who sing and those who dance shall say, all my fountains are in thee…."
(Psalm 87.7)

"Praise him with timbrel and dance; praise him with stringed instruments and
organs….." (Psalm 150.4)

GOD AHEAD

Work hard even in rain
Let your boots be dirty
Do not think of what
others think about you

Do not mind negatives
or criticism that can kill you

Tell yourself every morning
'God has given me a spirit
that cannot be destroyed
by any fool in this world'.

God ahead until you win.

"Truly I tell you, the tax collectors and prostitutes shall enter the kingdom of God
ahead of you....." (Mathew 21.31)

IN GOD NO SHAME

Be steadfast
be sincere of heart
Do not be alarmed
When distress approaches

Cling to God
Do not leave Him
Accept all uncertainties
Of your humble state

If you have trust in the Lord
You will never be put to shame.

"Both the man and his wife were naked, yet felt no shame…." (Genesis 2.25)

GOD IS COMING AFTER YOU

God's love turns
fear into faith
anger into patience
revenge into mercy
hatred into forgiveness

God's love changes
despair into hope
hostility into peace
pride into humility
selfishness into generosity

This God is coming after you
searching for you
You are loved by Him

Is your mind turbulent now?

Only realize it
and go to Him
God is coming
after you.

       Our God is coming
       He will not be silent!
       Devouring fire precedes Him,
       and a storm rages around Him.
              (Psalm 50.3)

LIGHT OF GOD

In God's light i want to live
In God's happiness i want to be
in God's mercy i want to grow
in God's light i want to see

I live in God's eternal shadow
I graze in God's heavenly garden
I sleep in God's sprawling mansion
I rejoice in God's everlasting love

With God's power I shall strive
With God's kindness I shall forgive
With God's blessings I shall believe
With God's wisdom I shall perceive

Be thou my Sight, Lord
Be thou my Light, Lord

Poet's Note :- The small i is symoblic so as to say that we have to be always without Ego to cherish the gifts of God.

Editor's Note :- It has been Hemangi Sharma's lifelong obsession to use small "i" in an effort to downplay the ego.

"And God saw the light, that it was good, and God divided the light from the darkness...." (Genesis 1.4)

"Thou shalt light my candle; the Lord shall make my darkness to be light...." (Psalm 18.28)

GOD MY CONSOLATION

God is my consolation
Why should I be anxious?
Anxiety takes my smile away

Joy is my dress which I try to wear every morning
I smile knowingly because a happy heart is cheerful

Hatred crushes the spirit
I want to love
All those who hate me

I want to dream deeply
Of peace and love
I want to express great joy

Joy is contagious

"This is my consolation in my affliction, that your word has revived me and given me new life….." (Psalm 119.50)

GOD ALONE

The 'Reality' is that which exists
within the sphere of the Almighty

All else is temporary
All else is thus an illusion

Had there been no Big Bang
God would exist still

Even when
Physical universe vanishes
God would remain

God is beyond all that is material
God is perpetual being
God is independent of materiality

God alone shall we adore

"Thou art great, and doest wondrous things; thou art God alone…." Psalm 86.10)

"Upon God alone doth my soul rest peacefully; from him is my salvation…." (Psalm 62.1)

I WANT TO SEE YOU, GOD

I shall extol you my God and King

I kneel down and look up
to the mighty heavens
and praise your from my lowly heart

I want to rejoice and shout for joy
I want to be meek and humble
You love a humble and contrite heart

You are a compassionate God
You forgive me though I don't deserve

You are faithful in all your words
You raise up all who are bowed down

O God reveal to me
Your holy face
I want to see you
I want to see you
I want to see you.

"For I want very much to see you, so I may impart to you some spiritual gift to strengthen you...." (Romans 1.11)

TRANSFORM GOD'S WORLD

God calls us to transform
our corner of God's world
to cultivate it into a terrain
of justice and peace

Too many are living
in parts of this world
where fear and violence
hunger and death
war and nuclear threats
are their daily food

Distress, want
deprivation, death
rape, stealing away
all that is precious
to a human being

Cruelty reigns in our world

What shall I do
Shall I silently watch?
I shall transform my corner
of God's wonderful world
and cultivate it into a terrain
of justice and peace.

IF I CANNOT DO THAT LORD?

Is there something God has told you
to do that seems just too difficult?

You can be sure that if He has called
you to carry out His will, He is going
to be faithful to accomplish it through
His Spirit living and working in you

So if you tell Him, "I can't do that, Lord
—what if I fail? " you're really saying,
"God doesn't keep His word."

And yet, our total expectation
should be in Him—not in our own
energy, ability, or experience

When you doubt God's trustworthiness
that unbelief alone will become a gap
in your spiritual armor, you can be sure
that's exactly where Satan will attack you

And you'll begin to doubt even more
about God's intent and character
His goodness—and all that distrust
will become a heavy load of baggage
you'll needlessly drag through your life.

"O Lord, I put my faith in you; take me out of the hands of him who is cruel to me,
and make me free...." (Psalm 7.1)

MAKE BEAUTY OF MY ASHES

Make beauty out of my ashes Lord
Make me feel nothing but hope
for the year ahead

Let my faith continue
to strengthen and grow

God, awaken the passion
inside of me to live
for You and You alone

God, set a fire
within me, a hunger
for more of God
and God's Word

I pray for steadfastness
please steady my heart
direct my steps and help me
keep my eyes fixed on You

Cultivate within me, Lord
a deeper understanding of love

Fill me with your love
Until I overflow

Allow my life to be
a reflection of Your love
to everyone I meet.

EPILOGUE

HEMANGI SHARMA

AS ANTONY THEODORE

I AM NOT FAKE

My dear poet friend
It is not a fake ID
Only my pseudonym
And I am not theoretical poet
I am a class one English poet
Though an unconventional poet
And an off the cuff instant poet
Name and fame I do not care
I am already published
In many languages
In many formats

Shakespeare was not dear
A follower like you poet
He was a poem in flow
You must have your own DNA
To become a poet of substance
I have been to a poetry academy
Where they stripped me nude
And now my poems they salute

HEMANGI SHARMA

AS DR ANTONY THEODORE

It was in the year 2007 when for the first time I noticed certain unusual activities in the internet. Several social media posts by different persons with different IDs had the same underlying pattern and digital footprint. It was quite unusual and strange. When I tried to follow some of these posts, I started receiving similar posts in my e-mail ID as spam messages. Although I found it quite baffling, I thought it could be just a coincidence.

Later in 2009 a woman started stacking me online and also over phone. I received a series of calls from a woman claiming to be Swapna from Bangalore. Sometimes the woman told me that she was working as an executive at Google India office, while at other times she said she was working at Facebook. The woman started calling me from different phone numbers, each time giving a different name such as Swapna, Jyoti, Kiran, Savita etc. It was quite obvious that it was the same woman, since the voice, accent, style and intonation was the same. It was also obvious that she was stalking me for an ulterior motive, since a Google or Facebook executive would have little to do with someone like me who had hardly any presence on social media.

During the years 2011 and 2012 there was a marked reduction in the stalking activity of this woman. So I had largely forgotten aouut those spam calls and messages. But then suddenly in September 2013 a woman named Chitrangdha K Ganesh sent me a message on Poemhunter website. The title of her message read "I am bowled over by your poetic skills". It was very perplexing. I

In August 2013 I had exposed certain fraudulent activities in the online Poemhunter Poetry Competition, in which I was a participant. I found that out of the 100 poems reaching the final, 37 appeared to be the works of same person. The poems showed exquisite craftsmanship and were on wide ranging topics. But all these 37 poems had a typical signature style. Many of these poems had been submitted by poets with similar names such as Prem Kumar, Prem Jyot, Prem123 etc. I had lodged a written complaint with Poemhunter.com website regarding such fraud, but received no response.

When I received the mail from Chitrangdha initially I thought as if the sender had some divine connection with me. But immediately I remembered the Poemhunter fraud, and thought this woman could be connected with that episode. Either the woman herself was the fraudster, or maybe some Poemhunter staff investigating the fraud. So I was wary of disclosing any details about me to this woman.

Although initially I avoided the woman, she kept on sending me her e-mail IDs and mobile numbers, requesting me to share my contact details. Although I was wary of the woman, finally curiosity got the better of me. I did some online chatting with the woman on Poemhunter platform. She introduced herself to me as a freelance worker in the field of advertisement and tourism. However after some time she started contradicting her own statements. Sometimes she said she was a researcher, a student, and IT professional or even a journalist. Sometimes she said she was married, and sometimes unmarried. Sometimes she said she was 39 years old, and at other times 33 or 43.

In April-May 2014 "Chitrangdha" obtained from me my mobile number and called me. In her very first call she told me about her life-long desire to study the Rg Veda and Qu'ran. She also told me that one day she would like to come to my house to study the Veda and Qu'ran with me. I found it quite surprising. Because ever since my childhood I had an unusual interest in the scriptures, and I had particular fascination for the rhythmic mantras of Rg Veda and Sama Veda as well as for the melodious Ayats of Quran as rendered by the Muezzins in mosques.

I developed a very intimate online relationship with this Chitrangdha. She was the first person with whom I had any personal chats online. She exchanged hundreds of messages with me via Facebook, WhatsApp, Poemhunter, SMS and other media. Sometimes she would call me up to ten times in a day. Often she told me that it was her life-long desire to come to my house and spend the rest of her life with me. I found t very strange. I suspected of a past life connection with her.

On June 5, 2015 Chitrangdha revealed to me that her actual name was Hemangi Sharma, and that she was a student at National Institute of Rural Development, Hyderabad. She also admitted that she had been trolling me since 2009 under a series of fake IDs. She said she came to know about me from a person named Basant Kumar Rath, a senior police officer posted in Jammu. This Basant Rath was my childhood friend and had studied with me in the same class up to university level. Hemangi Sharma aka Chitrangdha had been born and brought up in Jammu before she moved to Bangalore and Hyderabad for job.

In July 2015 I met Hemangi Sharma at her office in Hyderabad. She had invited me to participate in the annual convocation ceremony of her institute. She had booked a room for me in her office guest house. I spent two days with her. During those two days she shared with me her life story. She also discussed the hidden secrets of various world scriptures including the Bible and the Qu'ran. The religious philosophies that Hemangi Sharma discussed with me are the same that Antony Theodore has described in detail in his Christian poems.

When I met Hemangi Sharma in person she did not admit that she was Antony Theodore. But she admitted that she had hundreds of fake IDs. She showed me how she had created multiple Ids by using different mobile phones and SIM cards. But when I asked her to open Chitrangdha's e-mail, she said she had forgotten Chitra's password. When I asked her why she had opened so many fake IDs, she said that she had worked as a marketing executive at Google and Facebook, and that sending spam advertisements to unsuspecting customers was part of her lucrative corporate job. She also said that she had got fed up with that kind of artificial and unethical job, and therefore she had quit the job to pursue a career in rural development.

Initially Hemangi Sharma had shared with me those IDs through whch she had been sending spam mails. But after I came back from Hyderabad, Hemangi Sharma gradually revealed to me her other IDs under which she had posted thousands of poems online. Then only I realised Hemangi Sharma's true stature as a world class poet. I was surprised that she had not published even a single poem under her own name. All her poems had been published under hundreds of pseudonyms. After introducing me to her poetry, Hemangi Sharma deactivated her original e-mail IDs. So I was forced to correspond with her via her fake IDs. She discussed her poetry with me in great detail over thousands of messages exchanged through such fake IDs. And then one fine day she deleted all her messages to me. That left me with no evidence that she had indeed discussed her poetry with me. However I managed to save a few of those messages as proof of her correspondence with me.

Hemangi Sharma has uploaded thousands of her poems in different languages under hundreds of fake IDs. She is a multi-linguist with scholarly understanding of all major world religions. One fails to understand why a spiritual person like her would use so many fake IDs, which is clearly a criminal offence. But then strange are the ways of the devotees of God.

When Hemangi Sharma first started corresponding with me, I immediately knew that she was the mysterious person behind the hundreds of fake IDs under which she had uploaded her poems on various websites. However she admitted it to me much later, only after I relentlessly pursued her to know the truth. She did have the talent and creativity to write spontaneously in thousands of different literary styles. Hence tracing her identity from digital footprint alone is quite a daunting task. But there were certain underlying patterns in all her works. For instance, the most common element in her writings is her use of small "i" to denote the first person singular. She purportedly did so to underplay the individual ego in the creative process. In many of her poems she has expressed a desire to diminish her ego. But there is no plausible explanation for the use of thousands of fake IDs. If she simply wanted to avoid limelight, she could have adopted a single pseudonym to mask her identity, but instead she chose to have thousands. I believe that she wrote under fake IDs to completely dissociate her ego from the creative process. I myself had resorted to such a technique during my early student days. I found that the poems I had written under various pseudonyms were qualitatively much better than those published under my real name. Many of Hemangi's poems published under fake IDs are much better than the ones she directly shared with me.

Another underlying pattern in Hemangi Sharma's writings is her utter disregard for the conventional rules of grammar. Adjectives and verbs are created out of nouns, and vice versa, almost at will. Instead of "more childish", she will simply write "childer". For instance, in one of her letters to me, she wrote "love makes heart become childer". Among all her online avatars, I found Dr Tony Brahmin (Antony Theodore) as comparatively the most conventional one in terms of style. Still certain poetic freedom can be seen by discerning readers even in Antony's oeuvre.

Yet another frequent feature in Hemangi Sharma's writings is the liberal use of abbreviations and colloquial expressions. For instance she would write "RV Lovers" instead of "Are We in Love". You is abbreviated to "u" in most of her writings. Even mobile SMS texts such as Gn and Tc (goodnight, take care etc) frequently appear in her poems. She also uses past, present and future tenses in the same poem as part of the same dialogue between protagonists. Maybe this reflects her belief that time is an illusion, and that earthly concept of time does not exist at all in the realm of God consciousness. But what makes her art so special is that she makes such unusual expressions quite spontaneously. The reader hardly suspects that she is deliberately doing so.

In addition to "Antony", Hemangi Sharma has also adopted other interesting pseudonyms such as Lalitha Iyer, Dev Anand, Poet Poet, Sun Princess, April Pearl and a host of other IDs. She has used both male and female names, as well as names from different languages. She has used Hindu names, Christian names and Muslim names. Maybe she did so to identify herself with all humanity irrespective of artificial barriers created by gender, caste, race and religion.

But still she could have managed to do all this with 30 or 40 IDs. I really do not know what could have been Hemangi Sharma's real intention in adopting hundreds and thousands of fake IDs. Any discerning reader would have easily noticed the underlying pattern in the poems written by her under different IDs. But nobody pointed it out before I did so. I was the only person who lodged a written complaint regarding her fake IDs. Perhaps Hemangi Sharma deliberately did so with the expectation that someday someone would find out her real identity. Perhaps it was God's design that I would become that person. Or maybe it was Hemangi Sharma's own mysterious design – who knows?

Hemangi had frequently expressed to me her desire to open a school for underprivileged children, and also to adopt a baby girl with my financial support. She wanted to have an unconventional school, which would be completely free from the curriculum of rote learning. She told me that she wanted me as the Mentor of her "school". I do not know what exactly was in her mind. I asked her to explain to me her idea of "mentor". But she was evasive in her answers. However, from the very beginning of her interactions with me she clearly told me about her disapproval of abortion of foetuses. Protection of children and their precious childhood was her topmost priority, and it took up bulk of her conversations with me. She said she had left her lucrative corporate job to take up the study of rural development solely for the purpose of empowering vulnerable women and underprivileged children. But that still does not explain her thousands of fake IDs and deliberate lies. Why should a spiritual person tell such lies?

Hopefully Hemangi Sharma (Antony Theodore) herself will one day provide answers to all these unanswered questions.

Tapan Kumar Pradhan

A BRIEF HISTORY OF PSALMS

Out of the 1189 chapters in Holy Bible, the Psalms alone contain 150. Thus Psalms are the longest book of Christian scripture. They form a very important part of both the Old and New Testament. The original psalms were all composed in poetry form, in lyrical stanzas having metrical composition. But in subsequent translations they became prose sentences, thereby largely losing their original melodious charm. Originally psalms were designed chiefly for singing devotional praises to God, but modern day psalms are known more for conveying certain philosophical truths or the spiritual way of life.

There is no clear historical evidence or scholastic consensus regarding the origin of psalms. Most likely individual psalms were composed by different poets in different countries during different periods. According to Islamic traditions, divine knowledge got revealed to mankind during different ages in different forms through different messengers, such as Psalms through David, Torah through Moses, Bible through Jesus and Qu'ran through Muhammed. A majority of the psalms have been attributed to King David, while the next major attribution is to King Solomon. However it is not known whether the kings composed the psalms themselves or whether their salaried court poets and musicians did so. Before 15th century AD there was no formal system of crediting creative works to their original composers. Hence compositions by courtiers were often attributed to the kings who commissioned their composition.

According to historians, most of the psalms appear to have originated in the ancient Kingdom of Judah. And according to legends, the psalms were first revealed to King David (who ruled Judah and Israel between 1010 – 970 BC) as a divine inspiration. Originally the psalms were said to be sung in the temples of Jerusalem as a part of ritual worshipping of God. However, the First Temple of Jerusalem was constructed only around 950 BC by King Solomon who was the son and successor of David. Before the construction of this temple, that place used to host the Tabernacle (tent of worship). The Tabernacle had been first constructed by Moses on Mount

Sinai, and it contained an altar of worship, space for communal eating and various spiritual insignia such as an emblem of the Ark etc. The tabernacle had been used by Israelites for holy congregation and ritual worshipping of their God Yahweh. But daily rituals at the tabernacle did not contain any musical performance, although there was burning of incense sticks, ceremonial meal offerings, confessions and various sacrifices at its altar. Therefore, although the original Psalms might have been first revealed to David, most likely they were musically composed in prayer format during Solomon's reign for ritual singing at the First Temple. There is scriptural evidence of musical celebrations in the First Temple. The Second Temple of the Jews, which was constructed by Zerubbabel, Cyrus, Darius and Herod over various time periods between 526 BC and 12 BC, shows evidence of ritual singing. Both priests and laity, as well as men and women, took part in Psalm recitations, which included group performances and chorus. According to several scholars, such group singing at Second Temple in Jerusalem generated many of the later day psalms.

Originally the Psalms were sung by Jewish Levite priests inside temples of worship at Temple Mount in Old City of Jerusalem. Singing was done as per exact instructions contained in each verse. Levite priests were the patrilineal descendants of Levi, the third son of Jacob and Leah. They were the original privileged singers of psalms, which used to be orally passed down through generations. Priests used to sing them only at sacred places on specific occasions. However, later on they were written down in various anthologies, and were used widely for personal as well as communal prayers. They were recited in traditional Jewish and Christian worship during daily morning and evening prayers, as well as during special occasions like festivals, fasting and burial services. During early spread of Christianity the Bishops were expected to be able to recite the entire Book of Psalm from memory. But as original Christianity got divided into various sects and denominations like Catholic, Protestant, Orthodox, Lutheran, Presbytarian etc, the method of psalm recitation started differing from church to church. At present some conservative denominations such as Presbytarian Reformed Church sing only a small number of specific psalms in their worship and shun rest of the hymns.

Modern day Psalms can be classified into several types – e.g. Hymns (praises to God), Laments (description of suffering and petition for help), Royal Psalms (description of events in kings' lives), Thanksgiving (for deliverance from disasters), Wisdom (philosophical insights) and Pilgrimage (sung by pilgrims during journeys) etc. Different categories of psalms are preferred for different occasions. Some churches arrange daily oral recitation of the psalms theme-wise, according to corresponding days of the month. Many other churches prefer metrical composition of psalms for musical rendering with elaborate instrumental accompaniment. Most Catholic churches arrange ceremonial chanting of the verses by which the entire Book of Psalm is recited in a one-week or two-week cycle. The Catholic tradition has three principal modes of recitation – e.g. Direct (all present sing the entire psalm), Antiphonal (two sections of singers chant alternate verses) and Responsorial (after the main singer sings one verse, the audience responds). This is similar to many Eastern musical and liturgical traditions such as Sama Veda chanting.

Psalm chanting was initially confined to a closed circle of Levite priests, who used a fixed melodic formula for each psalm verse, known as the psalm tone. The original Jewish practice was to recite them at fixed prayer hours in a day, such as morning, noon, evening and midnight prayers. But after the advent of Christianity psalm recitation gradually spread to the common people or laity. Early Catholics maintained the Jewish tradition of reciting at fixed hours. But unlike the Levites, they conducted psalm recitation for private prayers at home also. The timing of recitation was also changed to seven fixed prayer hours – e.g. on waking up, at lighting of lamp in evening, at bedtime, midnight and at the third, sixth and ninth hours of the day. However, since original Psalms were available mostly in Latin versions, they gradually became less popular during Middle Ages, when knowledge of Latin language had greatly declined among lay people. Mass recitation of psalms by common people became widespread again after 18th century when English translations of the Book of Psalm became easily available. Until the 1960s the Catholics used to recite the Book of Psalms in a one-week cycle (rarely two-week) with a daily recitation of 25 psalms. In 1974 the official Breviary released by the Vatican prescribed

Psalm recitation in a four-week cycle. However monastics recite it in one-week, two-week or other convenient cycles as per the tradition in their respective denominations.

Psalms were originally designed to be sung to music as prayer offerings to God. In that respect they are similar to the Sama chanting of Vedic mantras. Just like psalms have a written form for reading, and a musical notation for hearing, similarly Vedic mantras have metrical composition in the form of Rk (ऋक्) as well as musical scores in the form of Sama (साम). Just like psalms have explicit directions for musical chorus and orchestra, the Sama chants have elaborate notations for melodious singing along with instrumental accompaniment. It is quite possible therefore that modern psalms originated from the ancient Sama Veda chanting, since all scriptures appear to have the same hoary divine origin. Bhagavad Gita (verse 10.22) extolls Sama as the highest of all Vedas, thereby indicating that devotion and surrender are considered higher virtues than knowledge, discipline or physical efforts.

There are 1875 mantras in Sama Veda, while the total number of Psalm verses is 2461 spread over 150 song chapters. In Sama Veda many verses are repeated, thereby bringing the number of unique verses down to 1549. The psalms also have many repetitions, and therefore the total number of unique verses in Psalms and Sama Veda are comparable. The Psalms have been dated to 500 – 900 BC, while Sama Veda is believed to have been composed around 1000 – 1200 BC. The word Psalm has been derived from the ancient Greek word "psalmoi" which means instrumental music, while the word Sama has been derived from Sanskrit root "saaman" meaning song. Many Greek words have been derived from Sanskrit words - e.g. Duo (two from Dva (द्व), Treis (three) from Trayas (त्रय), Neo (new) from Nava (नव), Doru (tree) from Daru (दारु), Pater (father) from Pitr (पितृ), Esti (is) from Asti (अस्ति), Kentros (centre) from Kendra (केंद्र), Mus (mouse) from Mushika (मूषिक) etc. Hence it is quite conceivable that the word Psalm is a modification of Sama, and that psalms have been derived from the original Sama chants. Just like Sama mantras were chanted to invoke Hindu gods, the western psalms were musically performed only in temples to praise and propitiate God. Individual verses in both Book of Psalms and Sama Veda are linked to one another by various literary devices like sequencing (a verse carrying the theme from previous verse) and concatenation (adjacent verses sharing similar words and cadence). Just like Sama mantras, the Psalm verses also indicate the lineage of their singers, besides clearly indicating the prescribed time, place and method of their musical rendition, including the instruments to be used as accompaniment. The overall meaning imparted by a whole Psalm or Sama chapter is supposed to be different from the literary meanings of their individual verses. However, while the original Psalm notations are now largely lost through disuse, the traditional Sama chanting has been systematically preserved in India through its glorious oral tradition.

Since the focus is on the music and feeling, rather than on surface textual meaning, psalms have a wide range and variety of renderings. These differ from church to church. Psalms use various poetic devices like restatement, repetition, synonyms, amplification and opposition for the desired musical effect. This clearly follows the Sama Vedic tradition where the original Rg Veda mantras are "distorted" (विकार) through various embellishments (स्तोभ), transformations (विकृति), elongation ((विकर्षण), separation (विश्लेषण), punctuation (विराम), repetitions (अभ्यास) and meaningless word play to attain the desired melody and harmony. Both Psalm verses and Sama mantras contain detailed instructions for musical rendering – while psalms have superscripts, Sama verses have both superscripts and subscripts as guidance for singers and musicians. According to Mahabhasya of Patanjali there were thousands of different schools of singing Sama mantras in ancient India. Similar is the case with modern day Psalms, which have been rendered differently by different western musical traditions.

Renowned composers like Johannes Brahms, George Handel and Gregorio Allegheri have composed individual psalms into different popular tunes. Composers like Mozart and Vivaldi have combined several psalms into church choir.

REFERENCES

Aquinas, T. (2021). *Commentary on Psalms*, Aquinas Institute.

Bullock, C.H. (2004). *Encountering the Book of Psalms – A Literary & Theological Introduction*, Baker Academic.

Coogan, M. (2009). *A Brief History of Old Testament : The Hebrew Bible*, Oxford University Press.

Flint, P.W. & Miller, P.D. (2005). *The Book of Psalms – Composition and Reception*, Leiden Press.

Forbes, J. (1888). *Studies on the Book of Psalms*, T&T Clark, Edinburg

Gillingham, S (2013). *Jewish and Christian Approaches to the Psalms*, Oxford University Press.

Kugel, J. L. (1981). *The Idea of Biblical Poetry*, Johns Hopkins University Press.

Mays, J. L. (1994). Psalms Interpretation – A Bible Commentary for Teaching & Preaching, John Knox Press

Mitchell, D.C. (2012). *Re-singing the Temple Psalmody*, Journal for Study of Old Testament, **36**, 355-7

Mitchell, D.C (2015). *Songs of Ascents*, Campbell : Newton Mearns

Tate, M.E. (1984). *The Interpretation of Psalms*, Sage Publications

Yogananda, P. (2004). Second Coming of Christ, Self Realization Fellowship.

Westermann, C. (1989). *The Living Psalms*, T&T Clark, Edinburg.

www.ingramcontent.com/pod-product-compliance
Lightning Source LLC
LaVergne TN
LVHW010503200726
843506LV00013B/2509